The Best Kids Cookbook

DANIELLE KARTES

An Imprint of Thomas Nelson
thomasnelson.com

The Best Kids Cookbook

DANIELLE KARTES

of Rustic Joyful Food

CULINARY EXPERT FEATURED ON
THE KELLY CLARKSON SHOW AND *TODAY*

60+
Fun and Simple Recipes to Get Kids Cooking

Tommy NELSON

An Imprint of Thomas Nelson
thomasnelson.com

The Best Kids Cookbook

Published in Nashville, Tennessee, by Tommy Nelson. Tommy Nelson is an imprint of Thomas Nelson. Thomas Nelson is a registered trademark of HarperCollins Christian Publishing, Inc.

Tommy Nelson titles may be purchased in bulk for educational, business, fundraising, or sales promotional use. For information, please e-mail SpecialMarkets@ThomasNelson.com.

ISBN 978-1-4002-5113-1 (eBook)

ISBN 978-1-4002-5110-0 (HC)

Library of Congress Cataloging-in-Publication Data

Names: Kartes, Danielle, author. | Kartes, Michael, photographer. | O'Neill, Brooke, illustrator.

Title: The best kids cookbook : 60 fun and simple recipes to get kids cooking / Danielle Kartes; photography by Michael Kartes; illustration by Brooke O'Neill.

Description: Nashville, Tennessee: Tommy Nelson, Thomas Nelson, [2025] | Includes index. | Audience: Ages 6-10 | Summary: "Get kids cooking delicious food, learning key skills, building confidence, and having fun with this all-new recipe collection from Danielle Kartes, author and chef, known from her appearances on the Kelly Clarkson show and the TODAY show. This cookbook brings kids into the heart of the home and empowers them to explore, learn, and contribute"-- Provided by publisher.

Identifiers: LCCN 2024056523 (print) | LCCN 2024056524 (ebook) | ISBN 9781400251100 (HC) | ISBN 9781400251131 (eBook)

Subjects: LCSH: Cooking--Juvenile literature.

Classification: LCC TX652.5 .K239 2025 (print) | LCC TX652.5 (ebook) | DDC 641.5/123--dc23/eng/20241205

LC record available at https://lccn.loc.gov/2024056523

LC ebook record available at https://lccn.loc.gov/2024056524

Written by Danielle Kartes

Illustrated by Brooke O'Neill

Photography by Michael Kartes

Images used under license from Adobe Stock:

Image on page 1, copyright tbaeff; Image on page 2, copyright Mny-Jhee; Image on page 6, copyright this_baker; Image on page 7, copyright kwanchaichaiudom; Image on page 9, copyright zcy; Image on page 10, copyright Ivonne Wierink; Image on page 11, copyright New Africa

Printed in Malaysia

25 26 27 28 29 VPM 10 9 8 7 6 5 4 3 2 1

Mfr: VPM / Rawang, Malaysia / July 2025 / PO #12311062

To
Baby Warner,
Baby Caroline
& Baby Charlie

Contents

LET'S GET COOKING!

Hello, friend! I'm so glad you're here to cook with me. When we cook, the world opens up! We get to explore different tastes, find new favorites, and show love. Cooking is also an excellent way to keep our bodies and minds strong, healthy, and energized to run and play, think and create, and be the awesome people we were meant to be.

Even if you've never cooked before, you can create a delicious recipe right now. It's really not hard! Start with the simple recipes and keep going. In no time, you'll be whipping up a full dinner or impressive dessert. Confidence in the kitchen starts with just *starting*. Every dish in this book is designed to help you learn to cook in a way that's simple, tasty, and so good for you. And remember, you can't make mistakes while learning to cook, only happy accidents!

One more thing before you grab that mixing bowl. You might see ingredients in my recipes that you've never tasted before. That's a good thing! This is your chance to discover your new favorite flavor. Did you know you have to taste something *fifteen* times to really know for sure that you don't like it? So go ahead—be brave, take a taste, and see if you don't just love it!

Are you ready to have some fun and become a whiz in the kitchen? Check out my kitchen tips in the next pages, and then choose a recipe and get cooking!

Danielle Kartes

TIPS FOR BEING A GREAT COOK AND BAKER

1. **Always have a helper.** Ask a grown-up before you start cooking. I know it sounds fun to cook up a surprise, but it's important to cook with an adult helper to stay safe. And never use the stove, the oven, or a knife without a grown-up's help. This could be your mom, your dad, a big brother or sister, a grandparent, a cousin, or even your babysitter! Anyone old enough to drive a car is a great rule.

2. **Be adventurous.** Try new foods. Never tried a certain fruit before, and you're a little scared it might not taste good? Well, there's only one way to find out. Give it a try! One of the best things about cooking is all the new flavors you'll come to enjoy. And once you've tried something, try it again! If you didn't like the flavor of a certain veggie last time, try it again—you might be surprised what you like now!

3. **Prepare for success.** Before you start cooking, read the whole recipe. Then gather the ingredients and supplies. Next, prepare or "prep" the ingredients. If the recipe says you need a food chopped, diced, or sliced, do that before jumping in.

4. **Have fun.** Making tasty things can be as fun as eating them! Don't be afraid to get your hands sticky, breathe in all the wonderful smells, and dance to all the sounds you make as you bustle around the kitchen. Cooking and baking are a treat for all your senses!

5. **Keep your space clean.** Cooking delicious foods makes for a great time, but it's no fun to create dishes in a dirty or messy kitchen. The good news is that it takes no time at all to tidy up. Pop the ingredients back in the fridge and pantry. Wipe up that spill or those crumbs with a damp rag. Put the dishes in the sink or dishwasher. Now the kitchen is ready for your next creation!

HOW TO USE THIS BOOK
Meet Your Kitchen Dream Team

This kitchen dream team will show up from time to time with suggestions, tips, and answers to your kitchen questions.

Walter likes to get messy, mix things up, and lend a helping handle.

Broc is campaigning to be crowned Everyone's Favorite Vegetable. He makes a *Splash!* in ranch dressing.

Teeny loves to party. She does a mean slice and dice on the dance floor.

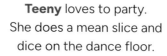

Scooter keeps it fresh and zesty.

Carole is ready to heat things up and show off her skills. She's not just for pancakes, you know!

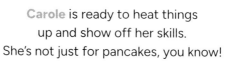

Recipe Symbols

You'll see symbols in each recipe that give you a quick heads-up for what to expect and ways to make the recipe your own.

Gluten-free

Hold the gluten! Many of these recipes are **naturally gluten-free** or **gluten-free adaptable** with a simple change. When you see this icon, check the ingredients list and tips for any substitutions.

Heat

It's hot in here! This icon means the recipe uses the oven or stovetop. Always ask an adult for help when cooking with **heat**. And don't forget a trusty oven mitt!

Sharp Tool

Watch those fingers. This icon means you'll need a **sharp tool** for the recipe. Ask an adult to help you stay safe with a knife, grater, or food processor. Or just ask your helper to do those steps.

Flip It!

Look here for recipe variations. You'll find substitutions to make the recipe allergy-friendly, ideas for other yummy flavors, or ways to customize for your family's preferences and health needs. This version of the dish may look a little different, but it will still be delicious.

Skip It!

If you don't like a particular ingredient, it's okay to skip it. Not up for spicy today? Leave out the chili. Not a tomato fan? Totally cool.

Using Seasoning, Salt, and Spices

The taste buds on your tongue can sense five types of taste: sweet, sour, salty, bitter, and savory. And just like our fingerprints, everyone's tongue is different. But your taste buds also change. As you grow, you'll discover that you like things you didn't like before. So when it comes to flavoring your recipes, your tongue is a true partner in determining how much seasoning and flavor is right for you.

You'll notice a lot of the recipes in this book say "salt and pepper to taste." That means exactly what it sounds like. Shake a little salt and pepper on the dish, then take a tiny taste to find out if you like the flavor or want more seasoning.

And don't be afraid to try the recipes that use other seasonings and spices! Most of these ingredients aren't *spicy* at all, but they add all kinds of different, delectable flavors that make each dish its own plate of joy. Garlic and onion powder might sound icky, but just a little in a dish adds a yummy, mellow flavor. There's a whole world of flavor out there to discover!

FOR STARTERS: KITCHEN SKILLS
How to Measure Ingredients

Dry ingredients

Flour, sugar, rice, and dried spices are all kinds of dry ingredients. Measuring cups for dry ingredients are metal or plastic cups with long, skinny handles. To measure dry ingredients, fill the measuring cup until a small mound of the ingredient rises over the top. Then use the flat side of a butter knife to level off the ingredient, letting the extra fall back into its container. This will form a flat surface at the very top of the measuring cup and make sure you are measuring accurately.

Wet ingredients

Water, milk, broth, and yogurt are wet ingredients. Use a glass measuring cup with lines and numbers painted on the outside. Fill the cup just up to the line of the measurement the recipe calls for.

Pinch

This measurement is exactly what it sounds like. Use your thumb and pointer finger to pinch a dry ingredient, such as salt or a spice. Then sprinkle the pinch into what you are cooking or baking.

Splash and dash

These terms mean the same thing: just a little bit. A splash of a wet ingredient, such as vanilla, is just a teeny-tiny pour. A dash of a dry ingredient, such as pepper, is a quick shake. When you see these words, just add what your heart likes and keep the amount pretty tiny.

How to Crack an Egg

Tap the wide part of the egg on the countertop. Then over a separate small bowl, gently place your thumbs into the crack and add just enough pressure to split the shell into two pieces. The egg will fall right out into the bowl!

How to Set the Stove for Low, Medium, and High Heat

Your stovetop has knobs that control the heat. They usually have the words *Low*, *Medium*, and *High* or numbers around the knobs. If a recipe calls for low heat, turn the knob just enough to turn the burner on. If the recipe says to use medium heat, turn the knob to the middle. And if you need high heat, turn the knob all the way around to *High* or the highest number.

How to Multiply a Recipe

At the top of every recipe, you'll see how much the recipe makes. If you want to make more than that, you can double or triple the recipe measurements. To make twice as much, use your multiplication skills and multiply every ingredient by 2. If the recipe calls for ½ cup of milk, use 1 cup to make a double batch. You can even make a triple recipe by multiplying the measurements by 3 if you have lots and lots of hungry bellies to feed. In a triple batch, ½ cup becomes 1 ½ cups. Got it?

How to Grease a Pan

Put a small amount of butter in the pan. Then smear it around with a paper towel to coat the whole pan.

How to Juice a Lemon or Lime

Carefully slice the fruit in half. If you have a juicer, twist the half over the juicer until most of the juice is out. Or give it a good squeeze with your hands over a small bowl, then finish by inserting a dinner spoon into the citrus flesh and twisting. Remove any seeds that fall in the juice before adding it to your recipe.

How to Prepare Veggies

Always wash your veggies by rinsing them under cold water before cutting and cooking. Then use a knife to carefully slice off the root or stem end. For most recipes, peeling is optional. Veggie skin is very nutritious!

How to Prepare Garlic Cloves

The papery skin on these pesky little guys can be tricky. Use the bottom of a spoon to smash the clove, and the skin will slip right off! Then trim the root end and dice or mince.

How to Prepare Onions

Cut the root and blossom ends off and peel off the papery skin. Then cut the onion in half to lie flat on the cutting board as you chop, dice, or mince. Chopped vegetables will be around the size of a nickel, diced veggies are a bit smaller than a dime, and minced ingredients are tiny like a grain of rice!

How to Chop or Mince Fresh Herbs

First, wash the herbs. If it's a tender herb like basil, cilantro, or parsley, roll the leaves into a firm ball, then slice. If it's a woody herb like rosemary or thyme, pull your fingers down the stem to gently strip the leaves. They'll fall right off in your hands.

How to Know When a Cake or Bread Is Done

This is a tricky one that needs some experience to get just right. When a cake is done, it is puffed and lightly golden. It pulls away slightly from the sides of the pan. When you insert a toothpick, the toothpick comes out with crumbs but nothing gooey. Bread is very similar. The crust will be a deep golden color. It will sound hollow when you tap the top. Use the recipe's bake time as a guide and adjust if needed.

How to Line Round Pans with Parchment Paper

Use a pencil to trace the bottom of a pan on parchment paper. Cut out the circle and press it into the pan. If you are lining two pans, layer two sheets of paper and cut them out together.

BUT FIRST! KITCHEN SAFETY

- Always cook with an adult's permission and get grown-up help with using the stove, the oven, a knife, or another sharp tool.

- Cook in short-sleeved shirts to keep your clothes away from hot pans and food. You can also roll up your sleeves.

- Wash your hands with soap and warm water every time you are going to prepare food.

- Anytime you use a knife, ask a grown-up for help. Then grip the handle firmly with one hand. With the other hand, make a claw shape to hold your ingredient. This keeps your fingers away from the blade. Then slice down slowly with a firm, steady grip.

- Unplug a food processor or blender before adding ingredients. Pour or drop ingredients into the container and never put your hand inside. Place the lid on tightly before plugging in the machine and turning it on.

SAY WHAT?
KITCHEN TERMS

Boil: Cooking food in very hot water with lots of big bubbles.

Brown or browning: Cooking food quickly until the outside turns a nice brown color, which adds flavor. Meat is often browned in a hot pan before it is fully cooked.

Chop: Cutting food into nickel-size pieces that don't have to be perfect shapes.

Dice: Cutting food into small, square pieces a bit smaller than dimes.

Fry: Cooking food in hot oil until it's crispy or browned.

Mash: Squishing food, like potatoes, into a soft, smooth texture.

Mince: Cutting food into very tiny pieces, about the size of rice grains. Garlic and onions are often minced.

On the bias: Cutting food at an angle instead of straight across so the pieces are longer and look fancier.

Sauté: Cooking food quickly in a little bit of oil or butter while stirring or flipping, usually for vegetables or small pieces of meat.

Set: When a gooey mixture cooks until firm.

Simmer: Cooking something in hot water that's not quite boiling, with tiny bubbles just starting to pop up.

Steam: Cooking food using the hot steam that comes from boiling water without letting the food touch the water.

Breakfast for Champions

Hold the gluten! Many of these recipes are **naturally gluten-free** or **gluten-free adaptable** with a simple change. When you see this icon, check the ingredients list and tips for any substitutions.

It's hot in here! This icon means the recipe uses the oven or stovetop. Always ask an adult for help when cooking with **heat**. And don't forget a trusty oven mitt!

Watch those fingers. This icon means you'll need a **sharp tool** for the recipe. Ask an adult to help you stay safe with a knife, grater, or food processor. Or just ask your helper to do those steps.

Mini Chocolate Chip Waffles

Prep time: 15 minutes | **Cook time:** 20 to 30 minutes
Makes 8 to 10 mini waffles or 4 to 6 standard-size waffles.

Who doesn't love a crispy and tender waffle? These waffles are extra special because they have extra protein from the Greek yogurt! Protein helps you grow and gives you lasting energy. So these waffles are a sweet treat for breakfast, but they also make a great snack for a hike or trip to the park.

SUPPLIES

Waffle maker
Large mixing bowl

INGREDIENTS

1 ½ cups all-purpose flour (or gluten-free flour blend)
2 eggs
½ cup plain Greek yogurt
1 ½ cups milk
2 tablespoons melted butter or olive oil
1 teaspoon baking powder
¼ teaspoon ground cinnamon
¾ cup mini chocolate chips
Pinch of salt
Splash of vanilla extract

STEPS

1. Ask your helper to plug in the waffle maker to heat up.

2. Dump the flour in the bowl. Then add all the other ingredients.

3. Use a large spoon or spatula to mix until the batter is mostly smooth. It's okay if it's a little lumpy because the lumps will cook right out. Don't overmix.

4. For mini waffles, pour $\frac{1}{3}$ cup batter into the waffle maker. Close the lid and watch that steam pour out the sides. *Sizzle!*

5. Cook your waffle until it's golden brown, about 2 to 3 minutes. Many waffle makers have a light that comes on when the waffle is done.

Super Syrup

Keep it simple with syrup and butter. Or get creative and make super syrup.

1 cup maple syrup + ¼ cup fresh diced fruit
1 cup maple syrup + ¼ cup buttermilk

This is a **dump-and-stir** recipe. You dump everything in the bowl and mix it all together.

English Muffin Breakfast Sammies

Prep time: 10 minutes | **Cook time:** 10 minutes
Makes 4 breakfast sandwiches.

Say goodbye to the drive-thru! You are a great cook, and you can create your own breakfast sandwiches to take on the road. And just like that drive-thru line, this recipe likes a little speed. You want to get everything warm at the same time so the eggs heat the cheese and Canadian bacon. Ready? Okay!

SUPPLIES

Toaster
Medium skillet

INGREDIENTS

4 English muffins (*gluten-free, if needed*)
4 slices Cheddar cheese
4 slices Canadian bacon
2 tablespoons butter
4 eggs

STEPS

1. Using a butter knife, gently slice each English muffin in half. Cook each muffin half in the toaster until they are all toasted.

2. Line up the bottom halves of the toasted muffins. Top them with your cheese and Canadian bacon.

3. Time to cook! In the medium skillet, melt the butter over medium heat. Crack the eggs into the pan. Be gentle so you don't break those yolks.

4. Fry the eggs until the white is almost set, then flip them with a spatula. For runny yolks, cook for 15 seconds after that flip. Cook the second side for up to 1 minute for a hard-cooked yolk.

5. Now assemble! For each muffin bottom, place the egg on top of the cheese and Canadian bacon. Then add the tasty top half.

6. If you're going to take these on the go or freeze for later, wrap them in parchment paper and then foil.

Blueberry Overnight Oats

Prep time: 15 minutes | **Fridge time:** 8 to 12 hours
Makes 4 servings.

Think oatmeal and a creamy, cool bowl of pudding all smashed together! Overnight oats taste like a creamy yogurt-and-berry parfait. It feels great to wake up with a delicious breakfast ready to enjoy on the way to school or at the kitchen table!

SUPPLIES

4 (8- to 10-ounce) mason jars
    or containers with lids
Mixing bowl

INGREDIENTS

¼ cup blueberries
1 cup old-fashioned oats
    (*gluten-free, if needed*)
1 cup whole milk
1 cup plain Greek yogurt
2 tablespoons honey or brown
    sugar
Pinch of salt
½ teaspoon vanilla extract
¼ teaspoon ground cinnamon
½ cup blueberries for topping

STEPS

1. Get those jars out and line them up!

2. In the bottom of your mixing bowl, smash the blueberries gently with a fork.

3. Dump the oats, milk, yogurt, honey or brown sugar, salt, vanilla, and cinnamon into the mashed blueberries.

4. Mix all ingredients well until the lumps are gone.

5. Load the creamy oats evenly into the jars and secure the lids.

6. The next day, top off each jar with the blueberries.

FLIP IT!

Instead of blueberries, mix in mini chocolate chips, strawberries, raspberries, peanut butter, or peaches.

Instead of plain yogurt, use flavored yogurt. Honey or vanilla is delish!

Fri-YAY Frittata with Sausage and Cheese

Prep time: 20 minutes | **Bake time:** 20 minutes
Makes one 10-inch frittata, about 8 servings.

Think of this as a delicious scrambled-egg pie without crust. Just cheesy eggs loaded with potatoes and sausage crumbles. Add a dollop of sour cream or salsa, and you're ready to eat. Yay!

SUPPLIES

10-inch oven-safe skillet
Whisk
Large mixing bowl

INGREDIENTS

1 teaspoon olive oil
¾ pound ground sausage
2 potatoes, diced
½ onion, diced
12 eggs
1 cup shredded sharp Cheddar or
    Colby Jack cheese
Salt and pepper to taste
Salsa or sour cream (optional)

STEPS

1. Preheat the oven to 350 degrees.

2. Add the olive oil, sausage, and potatoes to your skillet. Brown over medium heat, about 15 to 20 minutes.

3. Add the onion and cook until the onion and potatoes are soft.

4. Next up, whisk the eggs and cheese together in the large mixing bowl. Pour the egg-and-cheese mixture over the meat and potatoes. Gently stir to combine and season with salt and pepper.

5. Bake for 20 minutes, until the egg is firm and no longer glossy.

6. Serve with salsa or sour cream.

Browning means to cook until you get a nice brown crust on your meat. Browning makes the meat taste extra amazing!

Breakfast Piggies in a Blanket

Prep time: 20 minutes | **Bake time:** 9 to 12 minutes
Makes 16 breakfast piggies, about 4 servings.

Think of this little breakfast snack as the perfect tiny hot dog. It's already in its bun!
These are amazing for breakfast, lunch on the go, or even as a game-day snack. You
will be a hero in your family when you pull these toasty delights from the oven!

SUPPLIES

Rimmed baking sheet
Parchment paper
Pizza cutter or butter knife

INGREDIENTS

1 (8-ounce) tube crescent roll
    dough
1 (14-ounce) package cocktail
    weenies
2 tablespoons everything
    bagel seasoning (optional)

STEPS

1. Preheat the oven to the temperature stated on the
    dough package instructions.

2. Line the baking sheet with the parchment paper.

3. Unroll the dough on the clean countertop. With the
    pizza cutter or butter knife, slice each triangle of
    dough into two smaller triangles.

4. Grab a cocktail weenie and roll it up in one of
    the triangles. I like to start at the wide end of the
    triangle and roll away from myself to the pointed
    end of the dough.

5. Keep rolling until you've used all your dough. You'll
    end up with 16 breakfast piggies in a blanket.

6. Sprinkle the piggies with the seasoning, if you'd
    like.

7. Bake until the piggies turn a light golden brown,
    about 8 to 12 minutes.

Piggies are awesome
with a side of scrambled eggs.
Or if it's snack time, dip them
in **Honey Mustard**
(see page 69).

The Besty Best Buttermilk Pancakes *Ever!*

Prep time: 10 minutes | **Cook time:** 3 to 4 minutes per batch
Makes 7 to 8 medium-size pancakes.

These pancakes are not your average pancakes! They are actually *best friends* with butter and syrup. They are more wild and more fun because we put a touch of fresh butter in the pan, which gives the pancakes a crispy edge when they cook. So get out that mixing bowl. You are in charge of breakfast, my friend! Grab your helper and let's get crackin'—eggs, that is!

SUPPLIES

Large mixing bowl
Large skillet

INGREDIENTS

2 cups all-purpose flour (or
    gluten-free flour blend)
2 tablespoons melted butter
2 eggs
¼ cup white sugar
1 tablespoon baking powder
Pinch of salt
1 ½ cups buttermilk
Butter for frying

STEPS

1. Add all ingredients to your large mixing bowl and stir them up.

2. Heat the skillet over medium heat, never hotter!

3. Add 1 tablespoon butter to the pan.

4. Pour the batter into the hot, buttery pan with a ¼ or ⅓ cup measuring cup. Cook three pancakes at a time.

5. Watch closely. Once you see tiny bubbles on the surface of your pancakes, it's time to flip! Cook 1 to 2 more minutes after the flip. Feel free to turn the heat a bit lower if needed.

6. Repeat steps 3, 4, and 5 until all the batter is used.

7. Slather the pancakes with more butter, then add a drizzle of your favorite syrup.

Did you know that lumpy pancake batter cooks up nice and fluffy? So don't overmix.

27

Breakfast Burritos

Prep time: 20 minutes | **Cook time:** 15 minutes
Makes 4 burritos.

Ladies and gentlemen, boys and girls, *set up your stations*! Breakfast burritos are awesome because you make a little assembly line of breakfast yumminess. And you get to decide exactly how you like yours! I'll include a list of ingredients, and you choose what you want to use.

SUPPLIES

Large skillet

INGREDIENTS

4 burrito-size flour or corn
    tortillas
2 cups scrambled eggs (8 to
    10 eggs)
1 cup (8 slices) cooked bacon,
    crumbled
1 cup shredded cheese of your
    choice
1 ½ cups toasted Tater Tots or
    cooked hash browns
Fresh cilantro, chopped
    (optional)

Wrap leftover burritos in parchment paper and then foil to enjoy later.

STEPS

1. It's time to build your dream burrito! Lay your tortilla in front of you and add ½ cup of the scrambled eggs, 2 tablespoons of the crumbled bacon, and ¼ cup of the shredded cheese, and then top with ⅓ cup of the Tater Tots or hash browns. Add cilantro if you wish.

2. Now spread your ingredients out just a bit so they're not a tall mound. Just be sure to keep everything in the middle of the tortilla for easy folding.

3. Fold one side of the tortilla over the ingredients, then fold the opposite side over the first side.

4. Next up, fold in the end closest to you. Then *roll* to make the burrito!

5. Now, heat the skillet over medium heat. Have your helper place the burrito in the skillet, seam side down. The seam is where the burrito folds end.

6. Cook for 2 to 3 minutes. Then gently flip the burrito and cook the other side until golden brown. This melts the cheese and makes the burrito incredible!

7. Repeat the steps for each burrito.

Lunch Box Dreams and Snick-ity Snack Time

Hold the gluten! Many of these recipes are **naturally gluten-free** or **gluten-free adaptable** with a simple change. When you see this icon, check the ingredients list and tips for any substitutions.

It's hot in here! This icon means the recipe uses the oven or stovetop. Always ask an adult for help when cooking with **heat**. And don't forget a trusty oven mitt!

Watch those fingers. This icon means you'll need a **sharp tool** for the recipe. Ask an adult to help you stay safe with a knife, grater, or food processor. Or just ask your helper to do those steps.

Beany Cheesy Quesadillas

Prep time: 10 minutes | **Cook time:** 3 to 5 minutes
Makes one 8-inch quesadilla.

Tortillas are the perfect way to start an easy and tasty meal. Add a little
bean-and-cheese action and crisp up the tortilla in a hot skillet to take
lunch or snack time to the next level—crispy, cheesy, *mmm*!

SUPPLIES

Large skillet
Pizza cutter or butter knife

INGREDIENTS

2 soft-taco-size flour or corn
tortillas
¼ cup canned refried beans
½ cup shredded cheese of your
choice
⅛ teaspoon garlic powder
⅛ teaspoon onion powder

STEPS

1. Heat the large skillet over medium heat while you put together your quesadilla.

2. Lay out one tortilla, then spread the beans on top.

3. Next up, sprinkle the cheese over the beans.

4. Evenly shake the garlic powder and onion powder over the cheese and beans.

5. Place the remaining tortilla on top.

6. With a large spatula, gently transfer your quesadilla to the hot, dry pan. Always keep arms, clothes, and hands away from the pan.

7. Cook until the bottom tortilla begins to brown and the cheese melts, about 2 to 3 minutes.

8. Flip and cook the other side until toasted, about 1 to 2 minutes.

9. Let the quesadilla cool for 2 minutes. Then slice it into triangles with a pizza cutter or butter knife.

Dunkin' Dips

Dunk crispy quesadillas into sour cream, **Real Deal Sour Cream Ranch Dip** (see page 54), or **Pico Pico de Gallo** (see page 70).

Make as many quesadillas as the number
of people you are cooking for, or make extras
to prepare meals for all week long!

Gingerbread French Toast Sticks

Prep time: 15 minutes | **Cook time:** 8 minutes
Makes 24 sticks, about 6 servings.

French toast is a favorite in my house. It tastes like a holiday, but it's so fast to cook that you can make it just about any old ordinary Tuesday. Bring Christmas cheer to any day of the year with my gingerbread-spice version of this classic breakfast. Are you ho ho hungry?

SUPPLIES

Large bowl
Whisk
Large skillet

INGREDIENTS

6 thick slices stale bread
　(gluten-free, if needed)
1 ½ cups milk
1 cup heavy cream
2 eggs
¼ cup dark brown sugar
1 teaspoon vanilla extract

GINGERBREAD SPICES

¼ cup molasses
¾ teaspoon ground cinnamon
½ teaspoon grated orange peel
¼ teaspoon ground ginger
¼ teaspoon ground cloves
Pinch of ground nutmeg
½ teaspoon salt
2 tablespoons butter, divided

OPTIONAL TOPPINGS

1 cup crushed gingersnap cookies
2 cups prepared fresh whipped cream
Maple syrup, of course!

STEPS

1.　With a butter knife, cut each piece of bread into 4 sticks.

2.　In a large bowl, whisk the milk, cream, eggs, brown sugar, and vanilla.

3.　Stir in all those yummy gingerbread spices. Now we have our custard!

4.　Get a nice big skillet and melt 1 tablespoon of the butter over medium heat.

5.　Dunk about half of the breadsticks into the custard for 3 to 4 seconds. Be sure the custard completely covers the bread.

6. Fill the hot skillet with dipped breadsticks and fry them for about 2 minutes, until the bread is golden brown on the bottom. With a spatula, flip each stick and cook for 2 more minutes. Remove the sticks to a plate.

7. Repeat steps 4 through 6 with the remaining bread sticks.

8. Want to make stale bread? Simply leave sliced bread in an open bag on the countertop overnight to dry out.

For a **gluten-free** breakfast, skip cutting the bread. Whole pieces of gluten-free bread will stay together better.

⏫ **FLIP IT!**

⏩ **SKIP IT!**

Leave out the spices if you prefer plain French toast.

Chocolate Chip Granola Bars

Prep time: 15 minutes | **Bake time:** 20 minutes
Makes 18 bars.

Chocolate chips make excellent teammates. They are star players in cookies and sprinkle into pancakes with ease. In this recipe, they do some of their best work inside granola bars! These bars are a nutritious, sweet snack loaded with oats and dark chocolate chips. They are perfect for lunch boxes, playdates at the playground, and even a quick breakfast with a glass of milk (or coffee for Mom)!

SUPPLIES

9 x 13-inch baking pan
Large mixing bowl

INGREDIENTS

1 cup unpacked brown sugar
¾ cup almond butter or peanut butter
½ cup honey, warmed
½ cup butter, melted
½ teaspoon salt
2 cups old-fashioned oats
¾ cup shredded coconut
½ cup wheat germ
1 cup chocolate chips

STEPS

1. Butter the 9 x 13-inch baking pan. Or line the pan with parchment paper. Either way works great!

2. Heat the oven to 350 degrees.

3. In the large mixing bowl, add the brown sugar, almond butter or peanut butter, honey, butter, and salt. Mix well!

4. Now, add the oats, coconut, wheat germ, and chocolate chips. Mix again.

5. Pour the mixture into the pan. Press flat.

6. Bake for 20 minutes. Get help to remove the pan from the oven, and let it cool completely. Then slice into bars. Hot bars will crumble.

Use sunflower butter for a nut-free bar.

 **SKIP IT!**

If you don't like coconut, skip it and add ¾ cup more oats.

 **FLIP IT!**

Top with vanilla ice cream to turn this snack into a treat!

The Big Turkey Melt

Prep time: 15 minutes | **Bake time:** 10 minutes
Makes 4 sandwiches.

This recipe takes a typical, tasty turkey sandwich and makes it even *tastier*! The key is toasting the sandwich in the oven. Get your favorite rolls, layer them up with turkey and cheese, spread on tangy tomato mayo, and toast them—you're in for a tasty, tangy, toasty lunch!

SUPPLIES

Bread knife with serrated blade
Baking sheet
Chef's knife
Cutting board
Small mixing bowl

INGREDIENTS

4 Kaiser rolls or hamburger
    buns (*or gluten-free buns*)
1 pound sliced turkey
4 slices Havarti cheese
2 tablespoons sun-dried
    tomatoes
½ cup mayo
2 tablespoons grated
    Parmesan cheese

STEPS

1. Preheat the oven to 375 degrees.
2. Now slice the rolls in half with the bread knife or open the buns. Place the tops and bottoms on the baking sheet with the white side up.
3. Divide the turkey into four equal piles. Add one pile to the bottom side of each roll or bun. Place the cheese slices on top of the turkey.
4. Chop the sun-dried tomatoes super, super tiny!
5. Grab the small mixing bowl and add the tomatoes, mayo, and Parmesan cheese. Mix well!
6. Next, spread about 1 tablespoon of that delish tomato mayo on the top side of each bun.
7. Leaving the sandwiches open, bake until the cheese is gooey, about 10 minutes.
8. Get help to pull the hot pan from the oven. Smoosh the tops of the rolls or buns down onto the cheese and serve.

Add lettuce and tomatoes after toasting for a fresh crr-UNCH!

If you have a food processor, skip steps 4 and 5. Instead, process the tomatoes, mayo, and Parmesan until smooth.

If you're not a fan of mayo, replace it with butter or olive oil to make tomato-parm spread.

FLIP IT!

FLIP IT!

If you don't like olives, replace them with another ingredient.

Cheese and Olive Pizza Pockets

Prep time: 15 minutes | **Bake time:** 15 to 20 minutes

Makes 4 pizza pockets.

Crispy, cheesy, salty, and *yummy*! I've never met anyone who doesn't love pizza! These pizza pockets are so much fun because you can choose different flavors each time you make them. Today we are stuffing them with cheese and olives, but you can add pepperoni or sausage or veggies or . . . Let your imagination run wild!

SUPPLIES

Baking sheet
Parchment paper
Small bowl
Whisk
Pastry brush

INGREDIENTS

1 box frozen puff pastry
(2 sheets), thawed
½ cup pizza sauce
2 cups shredded mozzarella
cheese
½ cup chopped black olives
1 teaspoon Italian seasoning
1 egg
1 tablespoon water
Salt
½ cup pepperoni slices

STEPS

1. Preheat the oven to 375 degrees and line a baking sheet with parchment paper.

2. Now, take your thawed puff pastry and cut each sheet into four equal rectangles with a butter knife. This will give you eight pieces, a top and a bottom for four pockets.

3. Next up, lay four pastry slices on the parchment paper. Top each one with about 1 tablespoon of the sauce.

4. Add ½ cup of the cheese to each pastry slice and sprinkle the olives on top. Finish with a shake of Italian seasoning.

5. Now, top each of the four pastry slices with the remaining pastry slices. Make sure the edges of the bottom piece and top piece meet.

6. Press the end of a fork all around the edge to seal the pockets.

7. In the small bowl, whisk the egg with the water to make an "egg wash." Use the pastry brush to brush the egg wash over each pastry. Sprinkle the pastries with salt and place a couple slices of the pepperoni on top of each pocket.

8. Bake for 15 to 20 minutes or until the pastry is golden brown. With an oven mitt, remove the pan from the oven. Allow the pockets to cool a bit, then enjoy!

Caramel Apple Nachos

Prep time: 5 minutes

Makes 1 plate of nachos, about 2 servings.

Nachos with apples? Yes! It's a silly, simple, and sweet snack that you'll love to crunch on. And it has fiber and vitamins. What more could you ask for?

SUPPLIES

Cutting board
Chef's knife
Large plate

INGREDIENTS

2 medium tart apples (Pink Lady or Granny Smith work well)
¼ cup caramel sauce, warmed
¼ cup fudge sauce, warmed
1 graham cracker, crushed
2 tablespoons mini chocolate chips
⅓ cup fresh blueberries or diced strawberries
¼ cup chopped walnuts (optional)

STEPS

1. On the cutting board, slice the skin off four sides of each apple so you have a square.

2. With the apples sitting stem up, slice them thinly up to the core. Then slice on the other side. Discard the cores.

3. Arrange the apple "chips" on the large plate and drizzle them with your caramel and fudge.

4. Sprinkle the chips with the crushed graham cracker, chocolate chips, blueberries or strawberries, and nuts, if you wish.

Kids Charcuterie Board

Prep time: 15 minutes
Makes 4 to 6 servings.

~~~~~~

A charcuterie board (say *shahr-coot-er-ee*) is a plate or tray filled with delicious meats, cheeses, crackers, and other small bites. And it's so fun to share! Below, you'll find a formula for a wonderful charcuterie board, but make this recipe your way. What other fun snacks would you like to munch? Get them on there!

~~~~~~

SUPPLIES

Large plate

INGREDIENTS

4 ounces Cheddar or Colby Jack
     cheese cubes
8 pieces sliced turkey, rolled up
8 pieces sliced ham, rolled up
1 cup pepperoni
1 to 2 cups crackers

STEPS

1. Grab a big plate and arrange small piles of your cheese, meat, and crackers.

2. Add your extras: pickles, olives, sugar snap peas, tomatoes—whatever you fancy.

3. Get creative and use any of your own favorite cheeses, meats, crackers, and veggies.

~~~~~~

Add-Ons

Supercharge your charcuterie board with these add-ons.

1 cup tiny pickles
1 cup black olives
1 cup sugar snap peas
1 cup cherry tomatoes
Real Deal Sour Cream Ranch Dip (see page 54)
Hooray for Hummus (see page 57)
Zippy French Dressing (see page 66)

Fried Bologna
Meets Grilled Cheese

Prep time: 10 minutes | **Cook time:** 6 minutes
Makes 1 sandwich.

We've all had a grilled cheese sandwich before. These crispy, crunchy, buttery sandwiches are one of America's favorite foods for a good reason! Now, you may not have heard of a fried bologna sandwich, but I bet your parents or grandparents enjoyed them as kids. So we are combining two of the best childhood favorites to make a cheesy, meaty sandwich mash-up!

SUPPLIES

Skillet

INGREDIENTS

1 teaspoon prepared mustard
2 slices bread (*gluten-free, if needed*)
½ cup shredded Cheddar cheese
2 slices beef bologna
1 tablespoon butter

STEPS

1. Spread the mustard on both bread slices.

2. Sprinkle half the cheese over one slice. Lay your bologna on top of the cheese, then add the rest of the cheese.

3. Now put the other slice of bread on top, mustard side down.

4. Add the butter to your skillet. Heat the pan over medium heat until the butter is completely melted. Then carefully place the assembled sandwich in the pan.

5. Fry the sandwich until the bread is golden brown on the bottom side, about 3 minutes. Then flip the sandwich to the other side and cook for another 3 minutes, or until golden brown.

6. Repeat this recipe to make as many sandwiches as you like!

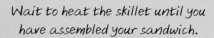

Wait to heat the skillet until you have assembled your sandwich.

Spicy Watermelon Fries

Prep time: 15 minutes
Makes 2 to 4 servings.

~~~~~~

This is the perfect summertime side. Three ingredients and lots of delicious fun! Serve alongside **Tangy Tomato Turkey Burgers** (see page 77) or **The Big Turkey Melt** (see page 38).

~~~~~~

SUPPLIES

Bread knife with serrated blade
Large cutting board
Large bowl
Citrus juicer

INGREDIENTS

1 small or personal-size seedless
    watermelon
Juice of 1 lime
1 tablespoon chili lime seasoning

STEPS

1. Ask a grown-up to slice the watermelon. Slice the watermelon from top to bottom into rounds, about 1 to 2 inches thick. The slices will look like dinner plates.

2. Cut the rounds in half.

3. Cut each half round into 10 "fries." (The "fries" are just slices!)

4. Place your "fries" in the large bowl. Sprinkle them with the lime juice and chili lime seasoning. Use a spoon to gently toss the melon until it's evenly coated in juice and seasoning.

FLIP IT!

Use a different fruit, such as a cantaloupe or sliced peaches.

Strawberry and Ham Bagel

Prep time: 10 minutes

Makes 1 bagel.

Chewy, creamy, savory, and fruity—this bagel sandwich has everything! Once you add sliced strawberries to your cream cheese bagel, you'll never go back.

SUPPLIES

Cutting board

Toaster (optional)

INGREDIENTS

1 plain or sesame bagel
(*gluten-free, if needed*)

2 tablespoons cream cheese

3 ripe strawberries

3 slices deli ham

STEPS

1. Use a butter knife to slice that bagel in half and pop it into your toaster, if you would like.

2. Spread the cream cheese evenly over the bottom half of the bagel.

3. Next, cut off the strawberry stems and slice the berries into 3 slices each. Lay them on top of the cream cheese.

4. Top the strawberries with ham and add the top of the bagel.

Dip, Drizzle, and Dunk

Hold the gluten! Many of these recipes are **naturally gluten-free** or **gluten-free adaptable** with a simple change. When you see this icon, check the ingredients list and tips for any substitutions.

It's hot in here! This icon means the recipe uses the oven or stovetop. Always ask an adult for help when cooking with **heat**. And don't forget a trusty oven mitt!

Watch those fingers. This icon means you'll need a **sharp tool** for the recipe. Ask an adult to help you stay safe with a knife, grater, or food processor. Or just ask your helper to do those steps.

Real Deal Sour Cream Ranch Dip

Prep time: 10 minutes
Makes about 2 cups.

Ranch is just a way of life around my house! I bet you love a yummy ranch dip too. With this easy recipe, you can make the *best* ranch dip with things you already have in your fridge and pantry. Get ready to dunk veggies, french fries, pizza, and so much more in this delicious dip.

SUPPLIES

Large mixing bowl
Whisk

INGREDIENTS

1 cup mayo
1 cup sour cream
¼ cup buttermilk powder
1 tablespoon onion powder
1 teaspoon garlic powder
1 teaspoon dried chives
½ teaspoon dried rosemary
½ teaspoon dried thyme
Salt and pepper to taste (I like
    a *lot* of pepper)
Buttermilk or milk to thin out if
    needed

STEPS

1. In the large mixing bowl, whisk all ingredients together. Mix for about 4 minutes, until the dressing is super smooth.

The dressing is ready to eat right away, but if it sits in the refrigerator for about an hour, it's even tastier! That is, if you can wait.

Hooray for Hummus

Prep time: 10 minutes
Makes 2 cups.

Hummus is a traditional Middle Eastern spread and dip. Recently, it's become a favorite in other parts of the world too, because it's *incredible*! Hummus is the perfect salty, savory, creamy add-on to everything from sandwiches, pitas, and crackers to vegetables and meats.

SUPPLIES

Food processor
Citrus juicer

INGREDIENTS

1 (15-ounce) can chickpeas, drained
Juice of 1 lemon
¼ cup olive oil
2 tablespoons tahini paste
1 small clove garlic
Salt and pepper to taste

STEPS

1. Place all ingredients in the work bowl of your food processor, and place the lid on top.

2. Blend for 2 to 5 minutes, until your hummus is as smooth as you like it. To make it even creamier, add water 1 tablespoon at a time until it's *juuust* right.

Hummus makes an awesome lunch box item. Pack pita or crackers, plus cheese, fresh veggies, and hummus for a flavor-filled, power-packed lunch.

Hummus Heroes

Add even more delicious flavor to your hummus with one (or more!) of these toppings.

Olive oil drizzle
Feta cheese crumbles
Sun-dried tomatoes
Olives

Did you know that tahini paste is sesame seeds ground up super smooth?

That's a lot of tiny sesame seeds!

Quick Ketchup

Prep time: 10 minutes
Makes about 2 cups.

Are you ready for the quickest, shortest, easiest recipe that will make you a kitchen superstar? This is the secret (sauce), my friends!

SUPPLIES

Mixing bowl
Blender (optional)

INGREDIENTS

1 cup tomato paste
¼ cup honey
⅓ cup white vinegar
½ teaspoon garlic powder
1 teaspoon onion powder
Pinch of ground cinnamon
1 teaspoon Worcestershire
    sauce
Salt and pepper to taste
¼ cup water

STEPS

1. Grab the mixing bowl and add all ingredients.
2. Mix until everything is well blended.
3. Dunk!

You can also use a blender to make the ketchup super smooth. Just ask your adult helper to give you a hand.

If you like a sweeter ketchup, add more honey.

Zesty, Zesty Italian Dressing

Prep time: 10 minutes
Makes about 1 cup.

This recipe makes me think of a yummy, crunchy salad or tasty sliced chicken. And both are delicious when drizzled with this dressing!

SUPPLIES

1 (16-ounce) jar with lid

INGREDIENTS

½ cup red wine vinegar or white
    vinegar
½ cup olive oil
1 teaspoon prepared mustard
2 teaspoons honey
1 teaspoon onion powder
1 tablespoon Italian seasoning
2 tablespoons finely grated
    Parmesan cheese
Salt and pepper to taste

STEPS

1. Place all ingredients in the jar and screw the lid on tight. I mean *tight*!

2. Now, shake!

I call this dance the Italian shake!

Fry Sauce

Prep time: 10 minutes
Makes 1 ½ cups.

Fry sauce is the classic sauce for french fry dipping and burger topping! This fry sauce recipe is sure to be a favorite. Enjoy this tangy, creamy sauce with **Steak Fries** (see page 126).

SUPPLIES

Small mixing bowl
Whisk

INGREDIENTS

1 cup mayo
1 teaspoon prepared mustard
½ cup ketchup
½ teaspoon onion powder
2 tablespoons dill pickle relish
Salt and pepper to taste

STEPS

1. Put all ingredients into the small mixing bowl. Whisk until smooth.

Strawberry Yogurt Fruit Dip

Prep time: 10 minutes
Makes about 2 cups.

Yogurt and fruit are a scrumptiously sweet combination. And it's just too much fun to dunk your favorite fruit into a fluffy bowl of dip. Serve your fruit with large toothpicks or small forks to help with dipping. To serve with strawberries, leave the tops on for an easy handle.

SUPPLIES

Large mixing bowl
Whisk or hand mixer

INGREDIENTS

1 (8-ounce) package plain cream cheese, softened
1 (8-ounce) container strawberry Greek yogurt
1 (7-ounce) container marshmallow creme

STEPS

1. In the large mixing bowl, whip the cream cheese and yogurt with a whisk or hand mixer. Mix until it's nice and smooth, about 3 minutes.

2. Add the marshmallow creme and mix for 1 to 2 more minutes. The dip should be fluffy and light as a cloud, with no lumps.

3. Serve with whatever fruits you love!

If you want a lower-sugar dip, skip the marshmallow creme. The dip will still be very yummy with just the cream cheese and yogurt.

 SKIP IT!

Use any flavor of yogurt—lemon and orange are amazing options as well!

 FLIP IT!

Zippy French Dressing

Prep time: 10 minutes
Makes about 2 cups.

Have you ever been to a salad bar? They were big in the '80s and '90s, and they all had French dressing! This dressing is like ketchup's really cool older cousin. It's tangy and loaded with tomato flavor, and it's delicious on salads, veggies, and so much more. My favorite way to serve this dressing is on a green salad with shredded carrots.

SUPPLIES

Whisk or blender
Large bowl

STEPS

1. Whisk up all ingredients in a large bowl. That's it!

INGREDIENTS

1 cup ketchup
1 tablespoon tomato paste
¼ cup honey
½ cup white vinegar
⅓ cup olive oil
1 teaspoon prepared mustard
½ teaspoon onion powder
½ teaspoon crushed celery
    seed
½ teaspoon paprika
Salt and pepper to taste
¼ cup water

You can also use a blender to make mixing quick and smooth. Plus, it's fun to see the ingredients swirl so fast!

Honey Mustard (Beggin' for Nuggets)

Prep time: 5 minutes

Makes 1 cup.

~~~~~~

Dip or dressing? Honey mustard does it all! It's one of my favorite sauces for dipping french fries and chicken nuggets, but it's also a zippy way to make a sweet and tangy salad. How will you enjoy it?

~~~~~~

SUPPLIES

Large mixing bowl or blender
Citrus juicer

INGREDIENTS

½ cup mayonnaise
2 tablespoons prepared brown mustard
2 tablespoons prepared yellow mustard
1 tablespoon white or cider vinegar
2 tablespoons honey
½ teaspoon ground black pepper
Juice of 1 lemon
½ teaspoon onion powder
½ teaspoon garlic powder
1 teaspoon dried chives or 1 tablespoon fresh chives
Salt to taste

STEPS

1. Mix it all up in your large bowl or a blender until completely smooth.

2. Refrigerate for at least 2 hours before serving. A great idea is to make it the night before.

Pico Pico de Gallo

Prep time: 15 minutes

Makes about 4 cups.

Think of pico de gallo as salsa's laid-back uncle! This chunky Mexican sauce is awesome for dunking chips, flavoring steak or chicken, and topping nachos. Make this sauce spicier with an extra jalapeño, or keep it sweet and mild by leaving the jalapeño out.

SUPPLIES

Cutting board
Small serrated knife
Large mixing bowl
Latex kitchen gloves
Citrus juicer

INGREDIENTS

8 medium ripe tomatoes
¼ white onion
1 clove garlic
½ bunch cilantro
1 jalapeño pepper
Juice of 2 limes
1 tablespoon tomato paste
1 tablespoon white vinegar
1 tablespoon olive oil
Salt and pepper to taste

STEPS

1. Remove the cores of the tomatoes and chop the tomatoes into ½-inch pieces. Add them to the large bowl.

2. Peel the husk off the onion and garlic and mince both. Chop the cilantro. Add all to the bowl.

3. Wearing the kitchen gloves, slice the jalapeño in half and remove the seeds with a spoon. Finely dice the jalapeño and add it to the bowl.

4. Next, add the lime juice, tomato paste, vinegar, olive oil, and salt and pepper.

5. Stir until all the ingredients are evenly mixed.

Jalapeños can burn your skin and eyes, so wear latex kitchen gloves when handling them. And always ask your adult helper for assistance when using a knife.

Mean Green Salsa

Prep time: 15 minutes
Makes about 3 cups.

Surprise your friends and family with a different, yet oh-so-delicious, *green* salsa! Instead of using tomatoes like typical salsa, this recipe uses tomatillos (say *toe-muh-tee-ohs*). They're like little green tomatoes, and the tart and sweet salsa they create is *muy bien* for topping enchiladas, cheesy nachos, or super burritos. Or go classic with some chips! This is what I call a "back-pocket recipe." I pull it out of my "pocket" often because it comes together easily and quickly and never lets me down.

SUPPLIES

Latex kitchen gloves
Cutting board
Small serrated knife
Food processor or blender
Citrus juicer

INGREDIENTS

1 jalapeño pepper
1 bunch cilantro
4 green onions
¼ white onion
1 (27-ounce) can
    tomatillos, drained
Juice of 2 limes
1 tablespoon olive oil
1 tablespoon white vinegar
Salt and pepper to taste

STEPS

1. Wearing kitchen gloves, cut the jalapeño in half and remove the seeds with a spoon.

2. Cut off the ends of the cilantro and the roots of the green onions. Remove the husk from the white onion and cut it into 4 wedges (use only 1 wedge).

3. Put all ingredients into the food processor or blender. Blend until the mixture is the *perfect* texture: smooth but with plenty of yummy chunks.

I'm going to keep this recipe in my back pocket so I can pull it out whenever I'm in the mood.

For an extra-precise chop, I like to use the pulse function on the food processor.

Dear Dinnertime, We Love You!

Sauce It Up!

Head on over to **Dip, Drizzle, and Dunk** and whip up a delightful sauce that will make your burger burst with flavor. Which will you choose today?

Tangy Tomato Turkey Burgers

Prep time: 15 minutes | **Cook time:** 10 minutes
Makes 4 burgers.

Move over, hamburgers—there is a new sheriff in town! These turkey burgers pack big flavor and are sure to be a new family favorite. The bull's-eye ingredient is tomato paste. Tomato paste is made by cooking down fresh tomatoes until they get nice and thick. We're going to mix that special paste into turkey meat to create burgers that burst with flavor.

SUPPLIES

Large mixing bowl
Large skillet

INGREDIENTS

1 pound ground turkey
2 tablespoons tomato paste
1 clove garlic, minced
½ cup grated zucchini
1 teaspoon onion powder
Salt and pepper to taste
Olive oil for frying
4 brioche or hamburger buns
    (or gluten-free buns)
4 slices cheese of your choice
4 leaves lettuce

You can also use ground beef, chicken, or even pork for this recipe.

STEPS

1. In the large mixing bowl, mix the ground turkey, tomato paste, garlic, zucchini, onion powder, and salt and pepper. Get your hands in there and squeeze. Mix until everything *juuuust* comes together. Be careful not to overmix into a sticky paste, since that will make tougher patties.

2. Now, press the whole meat mixture into a ball and place it on a flat surface.

3. Make your hand flat and gently karate chop the ball in half, making two sections. Then do the same thing to each half, leaving you with four even sections. With your hands, make each section into a ball, then press each one into a flat, round patty.

4. Heat about 1 teaspoon of olive oil in the large skillet over medium-high heat. Fry the 4 burgers for about 4 to 5 minutes per side or until they are fully cooked through.

5. Place the cooked burgers on the buns and build the burger of your dreams with your favorite cheese, the lettuce, or any toppings you love!

In a Flash Chicken Pot Pie

Prep time: 25 minutes | **Bake time:** 40 to 45 minutes

Makes 8 servings.

~~~~~~

Pot pie is one of those steamy, creamy dinners that taste like home. This version keeps the amazing real gravy but uses puff pastry for a crust shortcut. Make this for a cozy winter meal or any day you want a dinner that feels like a warm hug.

~~~~~~

SUPPLIES

Large saucepan
9 x 13-inch casserole dish

INGREDIENTS

4 tablespoons butter
2 tablespoons olive oil
1 medium onion, diced
4 carrots, sliced
4 ribs celery, diced
3 sprigs fresh rosemary or lemon
    thyme, leaves stripped
Salt and pepper to taste
⅓ cup flour (*or rice flour*)
3 cups low-sodium chicken stock
1 ½ cups half-and-half
1 cup grated Parmesan cheese
2 ½ cups shredded or cubed
    cooked chicken
1 cup frozen petite peas
1 box frozen puff pastry with
    2 crusts (*or prepared
    mashed potatoes for a
    gluten-free variation*)

STEPS

1. Preheat your oven to 350 degrees.

2. Melt the butter and olive oil over medium-high heat, then add the onions, carrots, and celery. Stir.

3. After the vegetables have started to soften, about 2 to 3 minutes, add the rosemary or lemon thyme, salt, and pepper. Stir in the flour. Cook for 2 to 3 minutes, until the mixture bubbles and the flour is mixed in.

4. Add the chicken stock, half-and-half, and Parmesan cheese. Simmer the mixture over medium heat and stir until it begins to thicken, about 3 to 4 minutes.

5. Add the chicken and frozen peas. Simmer for another minute, then turn off the heat.

6. Pour the hot, creamy chicken gravy into the casserole dish.

7. Completely cover the gravy with both thawed pastries. Press down gently along the edges to seal the pastry against the pan.

8. Use a butter knife to slice a few holes in the crust for air to escape. If you're feeling creative, make a fun design.

9. Bake 40 to 45 minutes or until the pastry is puffy and golden.

FLIP IT!

With a couple swaps, this recipe can become your new favorite **gluten-free** meal. Use white or brown rice flour and gluten-free broth for the gravy. Then top with thickly prepared mashed potatoes and bake.

FLIP IT! ⇅

This stew is delicious
over a piece of cornbread
as well!

Rockin' Red Beans and Sausage

Prep time: 20 minutes | **Cook time:** 30 minutes
Makes 4 servings.

Beans and rice are life! This recipe combines creamy, tasty red beans,
savory sausage, and veggies for the perfect stew to serve over rice.
Your family will ask you to make this over and over again.

SUPPLIES

Large soup pot
Cutting board
Serrated knife

INGREDIENTS

1 teaspoon olive oil
8 ounces ground sausage
1 pound andouille or kielbasa
    sausage
1 onion
3 ribs celery
1 green bell pepper
1 cup cherry tomatoes
3 cloves garlic
3 (15.5 oz.) cans red kidney
    beans, drained
2 tablespoons tomato paste
3 cups chicken stock
1 ½ tablespoons salt-free
    Cajun seasoning
1 teaspoon onion powder
½ teaspoon garlic powder
Salt and pepper to taste
White rice, cooked according
    to package instructions

STEPS

1. Place a large soup pot on the stovetop and turn
    the burner on medium. Add the olive oil and ground
    sausage. Break up the sausage into small bits as it
    browns.

2. Next up, carefully slice your andouille or kielbasa
    sausage into circles. Add the slices to the pot with
    the ground sausage. Stir as the food cooks to
    prevent burning and sticking.

3. With some help, dice the onion, celery, and green
    pepper. Cut the cherry tomatoes in half. Smash the
    garlic cloves with the side of your knife, then mince
    them into little bits.

4. Add the onions, celery, green peppers, tomatoes,
    and garlic to the pot. Cook for 5 minutes, until the
    veggies start to soften.

5. Now, add your beans, tomato paste, chicken stock,
    Cajun seasoning, onion powder, garlic powder, and
    salt and pepper. Give everything a nice stir. Cook for
    at least 30 minutes. The longer you cook the stew,
    the creamier it becomes.

6. Serve over cooked white rice.

If you like things less spicy, add less Cajun seasoning.

Cozy, Quick Chicken Noodle Soup

Prep time: 20 minutes | **Cook time:** 20 minutes
Makes 4 servings.

Kids, start your engines! We're on a race to flavor city! This delicious soup takes less than an hour from start to finish.

SUPPLIES

2 large pots
Cutting board
Chef's knife

INGREDIENTS

1 tablespoon salt
2 tablespoons olive oil
2 raw chicken breasts, cut into small cubes
1 large onion, diced
3 carrots, sliced into circles
4 ribs celery, diced
2 ½ cups elbow macaroni (or gluten-free noodles)
½ teaspoon turmeric
1 bay leaf (optional)
½ teaspoon dried thyme (or 1 ½ teaspoons fresh)
½ teaspoon dried rosemary (or 1 ½ teaspoons fresh)
2 quarts (8 cups) low-sodium chicken stock

STEPS

1. Fill one large pot one-third full with water, then add the salt. Bring the water to a boil over high heat.

2. In the other large pot over medium-high heat, heat the olive oil for 30 seconds. Stir in the chicken and cook for 3 minutes.

3. Stir in the onions, carrots, and celery and cook for another 3 minutes.

4. Once the water is boiling, drop in the pasta. Set a timer for the amount of cooking time given in the pasta package instructions.

5. While that pasta boils, you are back on soup duty! Add the turmeric, bay leaf (if you'd like), thyme, and rosemary to the chicken and veggies. Then pour in the chicken stock.

   Serve with crusty bread and butter. And have fun dunking it into the soup!

6. When the timer goes off for your pasta, ask your adult helper to drain the cooked pasta and set it aside.

7. Simmer the soup for about 10 minutes, until the veggies and chicken are cooked. The veggies are done when they are tender enough that you can pierce them easily with a fork. The chicken is cooked when it is white all the way through, without any pink when you cut a piece open.

8. Add the cooked pasta to the soup.

Simmer means to lightly boil. No giant bubbles, only tiny ones around the rim of the pot.

Abraca-Burger, Cheesy Mac!

Prep time: 15 minutes | **Cook time:** 35 minutes
Makes 4 servings.

~~~~~~

Are you ready for some kitchen magic? Say *abraca-burger. Poof!* You just
made that store-bought box of macaroni dinner disappear! Now it's time to
make a yummier, healthier version that will make dinnertime magical.

~~~~~~

SUPPLIES

Large skillet with lid

INGREDIENTS

1 red onion, finely chopped
1 tablespoon olive oil
2 tablespoons tomato paste
2 tablespoons Worcestershire
    sauce or steak sauce
1 teaspoon onion powder
1 teaspoon Dijon mustard
Salt and pepper to taste
1 pound ground beef, turkey, or
    chicken
3 cups wide egg noodles (*or
    gluten-free noodles*)
4 cups low-sodium beef broth
2 cups shredded Cheddar or
    Colby Jack cheese
2 tablespoons heavy cream

STEPS

1. In your large skillet, stir together the onion, olive oil, and tomato paste. Cook over medium-high heat until the onion is soft, stirring often.

2. Turn the heat to low and continue cooking and stirring for 10 minutes.

3. Stir in the Worcestershire sauce or steak sauce, onion powder, mustard, salt, and pepper. Stir and cook for 2 minutes.

   Congratulations! You just caramelized those onions. Sweeeeet!

4. Add the ground meat and cook for 5 to 7 minutes, until browned.

5. Add the noodles and beef broth. Stir to combine, then place the lid on and cook for 8 to 12 minutes, until the noodles are cooked through.

6. Carefully remove the pan from the hot burner and stir in the cheese and cream.

7. Serve with buttered toast.

Chicken Curry in a Hurry

Prep time: 15 minutes | **Cook time:** 20 minutes

Makes 4 servings.

This recipe is for the adventurous among you! Are you ready to explore some new flavors? Chicken curry is creamy, savory, and a teeny bit spicy, with flavors of coconut milk, garlic, and tomato. I've listed my favorite veggies, but you can switch them out for whatever you like or have in the fridge, and it will be just as tasty. Just be sure to ask an adult for help with the cutting. There's no need to wait for the delivery driver when you can make this fast, simple take-out-style curry at home!

SUPPLIES

Large skillet

Chef's knife

Cutting board

Large bowl

OPTIONAL TOPPINGS

Chopped cashews

Chopped cilantro

Juice from lime wedges

Sliced jalapeño peppers

INGREDIENTS

1 onion, roughly chopped

2 tablespoons olive oil

2 tablespoons Indian curry paste

1 tablespoon garam masala

4 cloves garlic, chopped

1 diced Fresno or jalapeño pepper

1 large zucchini, chopped

4 to 5 tomatoes, diced

1 cup sugar snap peas

1 pound chicken breasts or thighs, thinly sliced (about 2 breasts or 4 thighs)

1 (15-ounce) can coconut milk

Salt and pepper to taste

¼ cup heavy cream

Prepared rice

STEPS

1. Heat the large skillet over medium-high heat. Add the onion and olive oil and stir. Then add the curry paste, garam masala, garlic, and Fresno pepper or jalapeño. Cook until fragrant and caramelized, roughly 7 to 10 minutes.

2. Add the zucchini, tomatoes, and peas and cook for 3 minutes.

3. Remove the veggies from the pan and set them aside in the large bowl.

4. Now, fry the chicken until it's golden brown.

5. Add the veggies back to the pan with the meat.

6. Stir in the coconut milk and bring the mixture to a simmer. Add salt and pepper until you think the flavor is just right. Mix in the cream.

7. Serve over rice with your choice of topping.

FLIP IT! ⇅

Want to make this a vegetarian dish? Instead of chicken, add chickpeas and loads more veggies! Want to mix up the meat? Try thinly sliced beef, shrimp, ground chicken, or ground turkey.

 **SKIP IT!**

Don't love spicy? Skip the Fresno or jalapeño pepper.

FLIP IT! ⇅

If you don't have dried chilies, substitute one package of taco seasoning.

Slow Cooker Silly Street Tacos

Prep time: 15 minutes | **Cook time:** 2 to 4 hours
Makes 24 small tacos, about 6 servings.

With this recipe you, my friend, are getting very, very chef-y. The dried whole chilies in these tacos pack *big* flavor without adding spicy heat. Your tacos will taste like they could be served in a restaurant! You can find these chilies in the Hispanic aisle of your grocery store.

SUPPLIES

Chef's knife
Cutting board
Large slow cooker
Nonstick skillet

INGREDIENTS

4 tablespoons olive oil, divided
10 to 12 boneless chicken thighs
    (about 3 pounds total)
1 red onion, sliced
2 tablespoons paprika
2 teaspoons salt
½ teaspoon ground black
    pepper
2 tablespoons tomato paste
6 cloves garlic, smashed
3 California dried chili pods,
    seeds removed
1 guajillo dried chili pepper,
    seeds removed
1 cup water
1 package (24) street-taco-size
    corn tortillas
Your favorite toppings

STEPS

1. Crank that slow cooker to high, kiddo! Pour 2 tablespoons olive oil in, and add the chicken thighs and onion.

2. Now add the paprika, salt, pepper, tomato paste, and garlic.

3. Tear open the chilies, shake out the seeds, and throw them away. Add the seeded chilies to the slow cooker.

4. Add the water and cover the slow cooker.

5. Cook on high for 2 to 4 hours.

6. Turn the slow cooker off. On a plate, shred the chicken with two forks. Return the meat to the slow cooker to keep it juicy and hot.

7. Heat ½ teaspoon of olive oil in the skillet. Fry the tortillas over medium heat until they are soft and lightly browned, about 1 minute per side. Stack the tortillas in a warm place, such as the oven (turned off!) or microwave. For each new batch of tortillas, add ½ teaspoon of olive oil to the pan.

8. To serve, top the tortillas with the shredded chicken and any toppings you love!

Use two tortillas for each taco to help your tacos stay together around the juicy chicken. Just use two packages (48) tortillas.

Shortcut Pork Dumplings

Prep time: 20 minutes | **Cook time:** 15 to 30 minutes
Makes 40 small dumplings.

A dumpling, sometimes called a wonton, is a pocket of dough filled with meat, veggies, or both. These hot, soft, and chewy goodies are delicious and an absolute blast to prepare. Serve with soy sauce, chili oil, and steamed veggies.

SUPPLIES

Chef's knife
Cutting board
Large mixing bowl
Large pot
Small bowl

INGREDIENTS

1 pound ground pork, chicken, or turkey
1 egg
2 tablespoons soy sauce
½ cup chopped green onions
1 clove garlic, minced
Ground black pepper
6 cups chicken broth
40 wonton wrappers

For wonton soup, return all the finished dumplings into the pot of broth. Cook for 5 minutes over medium heat.

STEPS

1. In a large mixing bowl combine the ground meat, egg, soy sauce, onions, garlic, and black pepper. Get your hands in there and squeeze and squish until the mixture is even.

2. Bring the chicken broth to a simmer in the large pot while you prepare the dumplings.

3. Lay the wrappers out on a clean counter or baking sheet. Place exactly 1 teaspoon of meat filling on top of each wrapper. It'll be tempting to put in more meat, but don't do it!

4. Now it's time to seal the dumplings. Fill the small bowl with water. Dip your fingers into the water, then wet the edges of a wrapper. Fold the dumpling wrapper in half to form a triangle. Then press the edges together to seal. Seal 10 wrappers, then move on to the next step.

5. Place 5 to 10 dumplings in the broth, depending on the size of your pot. The dumplings should have room to float around. Simmer 4 minutes.

6. While the dumplings cook, seal the remaining wrappers. When the first batch of dumplings is done, remove them to a clean plate. Then cook the rest of the dumplings in batches until they're all done.

FLIP IT!

For a **gluten-free** meal, skip the wrappers and serve the meat filling in a lettuce cup, over rice, or over rice noodles. Delightful!

Hamburger Gravy and Rice

Prep time: 10 minutes | **Cook time:** 25 minutes
Makes 4 servings.

~~~

This was my favorite meal when I was a kid! But we used canned soups. Now that I'm a mom, I make the gravy from scratch. My boys love this meal just as much as I did growing up!

~~~

SUPPLIES

Chef's knife
Cutting board
Soup pot

INGREDIENTS

1 teaspoon olive oil
1 pound lean ground beef
1 medium onion, diced
2 cloves garlic, minced
1 (8-ounce) container white or
    brown mushrooms, sliced
Salt and pepper to taste
¼ cup flour *(or rice flour for
    gluten-free gravy)*
4 cups chicken broth
2 cups heavy cream
½ cup shredded Parmesan
    cheese
1 teaspoon dried
    (or 1 tablespoon fresh)
    chopped parsley
Prepared rice

STEPS

1. Place the olive oil and ground beef in a soup pot over medium-high heat. With a large spoon, break up the meat into small bits as you cook it for 5 minutes to brown.

2. Now add the onions, garlic, and mushrooms. Cook over medium heat until the onions and mushrooms are slightly tender.

3. Add salt, pepper, and the flour, then stir until the flour disappears.

4. Cook for 2 more minutes as you stir, then mix in the broth, cream, Parmesan cheese, and parsley.

5. Reduce the heat to low. Stir often and cook until the gravy is thick, about 5 minutes.

6. Serve the gravy over rice.

~~~

*The gravy is also delicious
over egg noodles!*

Speedy Alfredo and Garlic Butter Shrimp

Prep time: 15 minutes | **Cook time:** 10 minutes
Makes 4 servings.

Alfredo is a creamy, cheesy sauce for noodles. This meal feels very fancy, but you can whip it up in minutes when you use fresh pasta. Just boil the noodles and mix up the smooth sauce to make the perfect batch. Add a few garlic butter shrimp, and you are in for a dinnertime treat!

SUPPLIES

Large pot
Large skillet

Alfredo

INGREDIENTS

1 tablespoon salt
1 (9-ounce) package fresh long
　　pasta *(gluten-free, if needed)*
1 tablespoon butter
½ teaspoon (1 clove) minced
　　garlic
1 ½ cups heavy cream
½ cup shredded Parmesan cheese

STEPS

1. Bring a large pot of water to a boil and throw in the salt.

2. Add the fresh pasta and cook according to the package instructions. This takes about 3 minutes!

   While you're waiting for the water to boil, cook the shrimp.

3. Once the noodles are cooked, have your adult helper take 1 cup of pasta water out of the pot before draining the pasta. Set aside 1 cup of the cooking liquid in case your pasta sauce needs thinning. Set the noodles aside.

4. Now in the same hot pot, add the butter and garlic and stir over medium heat.

5. Add the noodles to the butter and garlic, then add the cream and Parmesan cheese. Gently stir until the cheese melts and the cream thickens. This takes only a few minutes!

Garlic Butter Shrimp

INGREDIENTS

2 tablespoons butter

1 pound peeled and deveined 16/20 shrimp

1 teaspoon (2 cloves) minced garlic

1 tablespoon fresh minced (or 1 teaspoon dried) parsley

Salt and pepper to taste

STEPS

1. Melt the butter in a large skillet over medium heat.

2. Add the shrimp, garlic, and parsley.

3. Stir the shrimp until they are cooked through.

4. Add salt and pepper. Top your pasta.

Fully cooked shrimp curls into the letter C. The surface turns pink and the inside will be white the whole way through.

Some Like It Topped

Add your favorite taco toppings to make your fajitas fabulous.

Shredded lettuce
Shredded Cheddar cheese
Sour cream
Hot sauce
Black olives
Green onions
Guacamole
Pico Pico de Gallo (see page 70)
Mean Green Salsa (see page 73)

Skillet Chicken Fajitas

Prep time: 15 minutes | **Cook time:** 20 minutes
Makes 8 fajitas, about 4 servings.

A fajita is like a delicious soft taco filled with bell peppers, onions, and meat.
My favorite fajita meat is chicken, but you can also use steak or pork,

SUPPLIES

Chef's knife
Cutting board
Large skillet

INGREDIENTS

2 tablespoons olive oil, plus 1
    teaspoon
2 chicken breasts (about
    1 pound), sliced into thin
    strips
1 teaspoon paprika
1 teaspoon garlic powder
1 teaspoon onion powder
½ teaspoon turmeric
½ teaspoon chili powder
Salt and pepper to taste
1 medium onion, sliced
1 green bell pepper, sliced into
    thin strips
1 red bell pepper, sliced into
    thin strips
8 soft-taco-size tortillas

STEPS

1. Heat the large skillet over medium-high heat, add 2 tablespoons olive oil, and sauté the chicken for 4 minutes.

2. Stir in the paprika, garlic power, onion powder, turmeric, chili powder, salt, and pepper. Cook about 7 to 10 minutes, until the chicken is completely cooked through.

3. Now, remove the cooked chicken from the skillet. In the same skillet, add 1 teaspoon of olive oil and cook the onions and bell peppers for 3 to 5 minutes, until they are tender but still firm.

4. Finally, add the chicken back in and stir to combine. Cook for 2 more minutes to heat up the chicken.

5. Just before serving, microwave the tortillas until warm, about 20 seconds. Serve the chicken inside the warm tortillas with the toppings you love!

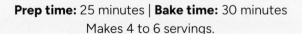

Lazy Lasagna

Prep time: 25 minutes | **Bake time:** 30 minutes
Makes 4 to 6 servings.

~~~~~~~~~~~~~~~~~~~~~~~~~~~~~~~~~~~~~

Everyone loves lasagna! Of course it's wonderfully tasty, but it takes a lot of time to layer everything up perfectly. So this recipe mixes the noodles in with all the other ingredients to save time without losing *any* of the scrumptiousness!

~~~~~~~~~~~~~~~~~~~~~~~~~~~~~~~~~~~~~

SUPPLIES

Chef's knife
Cutting board
Large soup pot
9 x 13-inch casserole dish

INGREDIENTS

1 tablespoon olive oil
1 pound lean ground beef
1 onion, diced
3 cloves garlic, minced
1 (27-ounce) can tomatoes,
    peeled, in juice or sauce
1 (15-ounce) can tomato sauce
1 teaspoon dried basil
1 teaspoon dried oregano
1 teaspoon garlic powder
1 teaspoon onion powder
Salt and pepper to taste
10 sheets no-boil lasagna noodles
    (*gluten-free, if needed*)
1 cup cottage cheese
2 cups shredded mozzarella

STEPS

1. You are makin' the sauce, kiddo! In a large soup pot over medium heat, add the olive oil and brown the ground beef.

2. Stir in the onions. Cook until the onions are tender, about 4 minutes.

3. Add the minced garlic, tomatoes, tomato sauce, basil, oregano, garlic powder, onion powder, salt, and pepper. Simmer for 20 minutes.

4. Break the lasagna noodles into big pieces, about 3 inches long.

5. Once the sauce is cooked, stir in the broken noodles. Now, pour the saucy noodles into the ungreased 9 x 13-inch casserole dish.

6. Preheat your oven to 350 degrees.

7. Drop the cottage cheese in small spoonsful over the top. Then cover with the mozzarella.

8. Bake uncovered for 30 minutes.

~~~~~~~~~~~~~~~~~~~~~~~~~~~~~~~~~~~~~

Serve with **Crunchy Caesar Salad** (*see page 117*).

Crazy-for-Coconut Shrimp and Rice

Prep time: 20 minutes | **Cook time:** 5 minutes per batch
Makes 4 servings.

Juicy shrimp with a sweet and crispy coating make a mouthwatering meal. Serve these jumbo shrimp with coconut rice and try dunking them in sweet chili sauce for even more fun.

SUPPLIES

Medium saucepan with lid
3 wide, shallow bowls
Whisk
Large skillet
Chef's knife
Cutting board

INGREDIENTS

Coconut Rice

2 cups jasmine rice
1 (15-ounce) can full-fat
   coconut milk
1 ¾ cups chicken broth
½ teaspoon salt
¼ teaspoon pepper
1 cup chopped cilantro
1 lime, sliced into wedges

Coconut Shrimp

BOWL 1

2 cups flour
1 teaspoon salt
½ teaspoon pepper
1 teaspoon onion powder

BOWL 2

3 eggs
¼ cup water

BOWL 3

2 cups panko breadcrumbs
2 cups shredded sweetened
   coconut
1 teaspoon onion powder
1 teaspoon paprika
Salt and pepper to taste

SHRIMP

16 extra-large shrimp (about
   1 pound)
2 cups vegetable oil for frying

FLIP IT! ⇄

*To make **gluten-free** shrimp, swap the flour for 1 cup of almond flour and 1 cup of baking powder and use gluten-free breadcrumbs!*

STEPS

1. In a saucepan, bring the rice, coconut milk, broth, salt, and pepper to a boil.

2. Reduce the heat to low and cook covered for about 15 minutes, until the rice is soft and the liquid is absorbed.

3. Get your dipping stations ready! In bowl 1, mix the flour, 1 teaspoon salt, ½ teaspoon pepper, and 1 teaspoon onion powder.

4. In bowl 2, whisk the eggs and water.

5. In bowl 3, combine the breadcrumbs, coconut, 1 teaspoon onion powder, paprika, salt, and pepper.

6. Now, it's time to dip! Roll each shrimp in the flour mixture in bowl 1. Be sure to fully cover the shrimp.

7. Then dip the shrimp into the egg wash in bowl 2.

8. Finally, press the shrimp into the coconut mixture in bowl 3, and coat completely. As you coat the shrimp, pile them on a plate.

9. Heat the vegetable oil in the large skillet over medium heat.

10. Fry each shrimp for 2 minutes per side and repeat until all the shrimp are cooked.

11. Sprinkle the cilantro over the top of the cooked rice. Fluff the rice with a fork to mix the cilantro in. Serve rice topped with shrimp and lime wedges.

15-MINUTE RED RAVIOLI

Prep time: 10 minutes | **Cook time:** 5 minutes
Makes 4 servings.

Every family has extra-busy days. This recipe uses premade ravioli for a speedy, saucy, scrumptious dinner you can enjoy any evening.

SUPPLIES

Chef's knife
Cutting board
Large pot
Medium saucepan

INGREDIENTS

1 teaspoon salt
20 ounces fresh ravioli
1 (25-ounce) jar marinara sauce
1 large tomato, diced
¼ cup fresh basil, chopped
     (or 1 teaspoon dried)
¼ cup freshly grated Parmesan
     cheese

STEPS

1. Fill a large pot with water and bring it to a boil. Shake in about 1 teaspoon of salt and cook the ravioli according to the package directions. Once the noodles are cooked, drain and set them aside.

2. While the ravioli cooks, you are going to jazz up your favorite jar of marinara sauce! Heat the medium saucepan over medium heat and pour in the jarred sauce, tomatoes, and basil. Simmer for 5 minutes.

3. Pour the sauce over the cooked ravioli and sprinkle the Parmesan cheese over the top.

To make the sauce creamy, add ¼ cup of heavy cream in step 2.

Oven-Fried Chicken Tendies

Prep time: 20 minutes | **Bake time:** 15 to 20 minutes
Makes 10 to 12 tenders, about 4 servings.

A chicken tender is a wonderful thing: crunchy, tender, savory, and home-makeable! This one is a real crowd-pleaser, so let your family members know they are in for a treat. You'll be very popular after setting a plate of these on the dinner table!

SUPPLIES

Large baking sheet
Parchment paper
2 medium mixing bowls
Whisk
Meat thermometer

INGREDIENTS

2 cups flour
1 teaspoon pepper
1 teaspoon onion powder
1 teaspoon paprika
1 teaspoon salt
2 eggs
¼ cup water
2 pounds raw chicken tenders
2 tablespoons olive oil
Salt to taste

These guys go great dunked in **Honey Mustard** (*see page 69*) *or* **Quick Ketchup** (*see page 58*).

STEPS

1. Preheat the oven to 400 degrees. Line the large baking sheet with parchment paper.

2. In the first bowl, mix the flour, pepper, onion powder, paprika, and salt.

3. In the second bowl, whisk the eggs and water until smooth to make an egg wash.

4. Next you're going to coat the chicken in the egg wash and then the flour mixture twice, to make a thick, crispy double coating. First, dip a tender fully in the egg wash, then dip it into the flour mixture until covered. Dust off any extra flour, then dip the tender back into the egg wash and back into the flour again.

5. Place the coated chicken tender onto the lined baking sheet. Repeat step 4 for each tender.

6. Drizzle the coated chicken with the olive oil.

7. Sprinkle the chicken with salt and place the baking sheet into the hot oven.

8. Bake for 15 to 20 minutes or until the meat thermometer reads 160 degrees when inserted in the thickest part of the chicken.

9. Use an oven mitt to remove the sheet from the oven or ask an adult for help. Let the tenders rest for 5 minutes before serving.

FLIP IT!

To make **gluten-free** tendies, swap the 2 cups of flour for 1 cup of almond flour and 1 cup of gluten-free baking powder!

Air Fryer Salmon Bites with Greeny Orzo

Prep time: 10 minutes | **Cook time:** 15 minutes
Makes 4 servings.

Salmon has to be everyone's favorite fish. Even if you think you don't like fish, you'll probably love salmon. It's meaty, flaky, and mild. Paired with these cute, creamy noodles, this salmon dinner is simple yet fancy enough for a special celebration.

SUPPLIES

Large saucepan
Air fryer (optional)
Parchment paper
Chef's knife
Cutting board
Large bowl

INGREDIENTS

1 (16-ounce) package dried orzo
1 ½ pounds skinless, boneless
    salmon, cut in 2-inch cubes
1 tablespoon olive oil
½ teaspoon paprika
½ teaspoon onion powder
½ teaspoon dried dill
Salt and pepper to taste
5 cups baby spinach, chopped
¼ cup heavy cream
¼ cup grated Parmesan cheese
1 clove garlic, minced

STEPS

1. Follow the package instructions to cook the orzo in a large saucepan.

2. Line the air fryer basket with the parchment paper. Set the air fryer to 400 degrees.

3. In a large bowl, mix the salmon cubes, olive oil, paprika, onion powder, dill, salt, and pepper.

4. Add the seasoned salmon to the air fryer basket and cook for 5 minutes. Flip, then cook for 5 more minutes.

5. When the orzo is done, drain and return it to the pan. Adjust the heat to low.

6. Mix in the chopped spinach, cream, Parmesan cheese, and garlic.

If you don't have an air fryer, no problem! Bake the salmon bites in a glass 9 x 13-inch baking dish for 15 minutes at 375 degrees.

Potato Wedge Nachos

Prep time: 10 minutes | **Bake time:** 40 to 45 minutes

Makes 4 servings.

Do you love nachos? They are irresistible! But what if we use some golden, creamy, tasty potato wedges instead of tortilla chips and *then* top them with your favorite nacho fixin's? Well, then we'd have a nacho-tater-tastic masterpiece meal.

SUPPLIES

Large baking sheet
Parchment paper
Chef's knife
Cutting board
Large mixing bowl
Large skillet

INGREDIENTS

POTATO WEDGES

6 to 8 medium Yukon Gold
   potatoes, washed
2 tablespoons olive oil
Salt and pepper to taste
½ teaspoon paprika

SEASONED BEEF

1 ½ pounds lean ground beef
1 teaspoon olive oil
2 teaspoons paprika
½ teaspoon turmeric
1 teaspoon garlic powder
1 teaspoon onion powder
Salt and pepper to taste

TOPPINGS

2 to 3 cups shredded Cheddar cheese
1 cup sliced olives
1 cup diced tomatoes
1 bunch green onions, diced
1 bunch cilantro, chopped
Sour cream
Salsa

STEPS

1. Preheat the oven to 375 degrees. Line a large baking sheet with parchment paper.

2. Slice each potato in half and lay the halves cut side down on the cutting board. Now, cut the halves into wedges about ½ inch thick.

3. Toss the potatoes in a large mixing bowl with 2 tablespoons olive oil, salt and pepper, and ½ teaspoon paprika. Bake them on the lined baking sheet for 35 to 40 minutes or until the potatoes are soft and golden on the edges.

4. While the potatoes bake, cook the beef. Heat a large skillet over medium heat. Add the beef, 1 teaspoon olive oil, 2 teaspoons paprika, turmeric, garlic powder, onion powder, salt, and pepper. Break up the meat and cook until it is browned through.

FLIP IT! ⇅

For a quick version, swap the fresh potatoes for frozen Tater Tots or french fries. Cook them according to the package instructions, then jump into this recipe at step 4!

5. Top the cooked potatoes with the beef, cheese, and olives. Bake for 5 minutes, until the cheese is melted.

6. Add all the toppings you love!

Hey, Dude! Tortilla Pizza

Prep time: 5 minutes | **Bake time:** 12 to 17 minutes
Makes 4 personal pizzas.

Bring hot, homemade pizza to your table for any meal with this quick variation. Just add sauce and your favorite toppings to a tortilla, and *hey, dudes and dudettes!*—you just made a perfect pizza.

SUPPLIES

Baking sheet
Parchment paper

INGREDIENTS

4 soft-taco-size tortillas
   (*gluten-free, if needed*)
½ cup pizza sauce
2 cups shredded mozzarella
   cheese

STEPS

1. Preheat the oven to 375 degrees. Cover the baking sheet with the parchment paper and lay out your tortillas on the baking sheet.

2. Next, spread 1 to 2 tablespoons of the pizza sauce over each tortilla, almost to the edge.

3. Top each tortilla with ½ cup of the shredded mozzarella. Then add your favorite toppings.

4. Bake the pizzas for 12 minutes, until the cheese is gooey and the crust is lightly browned. Or, if you like your pizza extra crispy, bake for 5 more minutes!

Topping suggestions

Sliced olives
Diced green bell peppers
Pepperoni
Crumbled cooked sausage
Chopped fresh basil or chives

Too much sauce will make the pizzas soggy. If you like lots of sauce, heat a small dish of extra sauce and dunk the cooked pizza.

Not-So-Boring Side Dishes

Hold the gluten! Many of these recipes are **naturally gluten-free** or **gluten-free adaptable** with a simple change. When you see this icon, check the ingredients list and tips for any substitutions.

It's hot in here! This icon means the recipe uses the oven or stovetop. Always ask an adult for help when cooking with **heat**. And don't forget a trusty oven mitt!

Watch those fingers. This icon means you'll need a **sharp tool** for the recipe. Ask an adult to help you stay safe with a knife, grater, or food processor. Or just ask your helper to do those steps.

Garlic Butter Broccoli

Prep time: 5 minutes | **Cook time:** 6 minutes

Makes 4 servings.

Broccoli gets a bad rap—likely because it's easy to overcook, and then it turns brownish green and smells a bit like a toot. But that's not fair! Veggies are so much more than "good for you." When cooked properly, they're just plain *good*! This easy recipe makes broccoli that is bright green, crispy, flavorful, and the perfect side to your favorite main course.

SUPPLIES

Chef's knife
Cutting board
Large pot with lid

INGREDIENTS

1 pound broccoli, washed and
    cut into florets
2 tablespoons butter
2 cloves garlic, minced
Salt to taste

STEPS

1. Pour water into a large pot until it is 1 inch high. Turn the burner on high and add the broccoli immediately. Cook for 6 minutes with the pot lid on.

2. Drain the water. Then place the pot over high heat for 30 seconds to evaporate any extra water.

3. Turn the stove off and add the butter and garlic. Stir gently for 1 minute, until the butter melts and coats the broccoli.

4. Sprinkle the broccoli with salt.

FLIP IT!

Other veggies are delicious with this recipe too. Try these:

Sugar snap peas
Cauliflower
Brussels sprouts
Green beans
Sliced carrots

Crunchy Caesar Salad

Prep time: 10 minutes
Makes 4 to 6 servings.

~~~~~~

This salad is creamy and tangy. Plus, chopping up heads of lettuce is so much fun!
Go fresh with homemade dressing or use bottled dressing for a quick version.

~~~~~~

SUPPLIES

Food processor or blender
Chef's knife
Cutting board
Large bowl

INGREDIENTS

CAESAR DRESSING

½ cup mayo
Juice of 1 lemon
2 anchovy fillets
2 tablespoons grated Parmesan
    cheese
Salt and pepper to taste

SALAD

1 head romaine lettuce, chopped
    into bite-size pieces
4 cups spring mix greens
½ cup grated Parmesan cheese
2 cups croutons
1 lemon, cut into wedges

STEPS

1. Place all the dressing ingredients in a food
    processor or blender and mix until completely
    combined.

2. In a large bowl, layer the lettuce and greens with
    the dressing and *gently* mix.

3. Next, top with ½ cup grated Parmesan cheese
    and croutons.

4. Squeeze lemon juice from the wedges onto the
    salad right before eating.

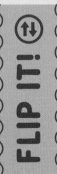

FLIP IT!

Want to skip the anchovies?
Use 2 tablespoons of capers instead.

 **SKIP IT!**

Leave off the croutons to
keep the salad **gluten-free**.

Just a Teeny Bit Spicy Carrots

Prep time: 10 minutes | **Cook time:** 8 to 10 minutes
Makes 4 servings.

We've all had vegetables as a side dish, sure, but have you ever had a *spicy* little carrot? If you like salsa, you will love these sweet and tangy carrots with a touch of heat.

SUPPLIES

Chef's knife
Cutting board
Large skillet

INGREDIENTS

8 medium carrots
1 tablespoon olive oil
1 tablespoon butter
4 dashes hot sauce
1 tablespoon honey
1 clove garlic, minced
1 tablespoon chopped chives

STEPS

1. Wash the carrots and slice them on the bias.

2. In a large skillet over medium heat, sauté the carrots in the olive oil and butter for 5 minutes. Stir occasionally.

3. Mix in the hot sauce, honey, garlic, and chives. Cook for another 3 to 5 minutes, until the carrots soften slightly.

You may peel the carrots for a smoother outer texture, but it's optional!

On the bias means on the diagonal. Cutting on the bias makes ovals instead of small circles.

Big-Time Berry Fruit Salad

Prep time: 10 minutes
Makes 4 to 8 servings.

~~~~~~

When you need a quick and tasty side dish or snack, think fresh. Pack this fruit salad in recyclable lidded plastic cups, and you have a wonderful travel treat or the perfect after-game snack for the team.

~~~~~~

SUPPLIES

Large bowl
Citrus juicer

INGREDIENTS

2 cups fresh blueberries
2 cups sliced strawberries
1 cup fresh raspberries
2 teaspoons honey
Juice of 1 lime

STEPS

1. Place the blueberries, strawberries, and raspberries in the large bowl.

2. Drizzle the honey over the fruit, then squeeze the lime juice on top.

3. Now gently fold the salad together, so as not to smash the berries.

Use any berries you like in this salad. They all work splendidly!

 SKIP IT!

If you want the salad to stay fresh longer, skip the honey and lime juice.

 FLIP IT!

Sunshiny Tropical Fruit Salad

Prep time: 20 minutes
Makes 4 to 6 servings.

The best part about fruit salad is that it's everyone's favorite! This tropical salad combines smooth and tart fruits for a salad that tastes like sunshine. Or switch up the fruit to make this *your* favorite fruit salad! Be sure to get some help from an adult with all the cutting and chopping.

SUPPLIES

Chef's knife
Cutting board
Large mixing bowl
Small bowl
Citrus juicer

INGREDIENTS

2 ripe mangoes
1 medium pineapple
½ cantaloupe
½ cup unsweetened coconut
    flakes or shreds
1 teaspoon honey
Juice of 1 lime
Pinch of salt

STEPS

1. Remove the mango peels and cut the fruit from the pits. Cut off the rind of the pineapple and cantaloupe, and remove the pineapple core and cantaloupe seeds.

2. Chop the mangoes, pineapple, and cantaloupe into large chunks, about one inch big. As you chop, place the pieces in the large bowl.

3. In the small bowl, mix the coconut, honey, lime juice, and salt.

4. Add the honey-lime dressing to the fruit and gently stir to coat.

If you'd like to add a banana, slice it on top of the salad right before eating. If you mix the banana in, it will get slippery and brown.

Did you know that adding lemon or lime juice keeps fruit from turning brown?

Kids Tapas

Prep time: 15 minutes
Makes 4 servings.

Once I brought my kiddos to a friend's house, and before dinner they put out a tray of small, munchy snacks: sugar snap peas, cheese cubes, sliced strawberries, and similar bites. We started this little trend at our house, and we never looked back. Pile all kinds of fruits and veggies, crackers, and cheeses onto a tray or in individual bowls. Then invite your family or friends to choose two or three items to start. These snacks are the perfect way to start a meal and get some extra fiber and vitamins!

SUPPLIES

Small kitchen knife
Cutting board
Tray

PICK-AND-CHOOSE INGREDIENTS

1 cup sugar snap peas
2 medium carrots, sliced into
   sticks
1 avocado, sliced in half,
   pit removed
2 ribs celery, sliced into sticks
1 cucumber, sliced
1 apple, cored and sliced
1 cup blueberries
1 cup grapes
1 cup raw cauliflower florets

STEPS

1. Arrange the snacks on the tray in piles that touch.

2. Crunch and munch!

Tapas is a Spanish word meaning small, savory snacks.

YUM!

Steak Fries

Prep time: 10 minutes | **Bake time:** 35 to 45 minutes

Makes 4 servings.

Steak fries is a hilarious name for french fries. These thick-cut fries are commonly paired with juicy steaks in Europe. Dunk 'em and dip 'em and serve 'em with burgers or chili too.

SUPPLIES

Baking sheet
Parchment paper
Chef's knife
Cutting board

INGREDIENTS

3 large russet potatoes
2 teaspoons olive oil
1 teaspoon seasoning salt

STEPS

1. Preheat the oven to 375 degrees. Line the baking sheet with parchment paper.

2. Wash the potatoes. Scrub the skin with a dishcloth or vegetable brush under water.

3. Slice each potato in half and lay the halves cut side down on the cutting board. Now, cut the halves into wedges about ½ inch thick.

4. Place the cut potatoes on the lined baking sheet and drizzle the olive oil over the top. Sprinkle the potatoes with the seasoning salt.

5. Get your hands in there and mix up the potatoes until they are evenly coated in oil and salt.

6. Bake for 35 to 45 minutes, until the fries are crispy and golden.

Serve with **Fry Sauce** *(see page 62).*

Sweet Treats

Hold the gluten! Many of these recipes are **naturally gluten-free** or **gluten-free adaptable** with a simple change. When you see this icon, check the ingredients list and tips for any substitutions.

It's hot in here! This icon means the recipe uses the oven or stovetop. Always ask an adult for help when cooking with **heat**. And don't forget a trusty oven mitt!

Watch those fingers. This icon means you'll need a **sharp tool** for the recipe. Ask an adult to help you stay safe with a knife, grater, or food processor. Or just ask your helper to do those steps.

Apple Cinna-Mini Scones

Prep time: 20 minutes | **Bake time:** 15 to 20 minutes
Makes 16 scones.

The only thing better than a buttery, crumbly scone is a mini scone, of course! These little apple scones are sweet, satisfying, and easy to whip up.

SUPPLIES

Baking sheet
Parchment paper
Small kitchen knife
Cutting board
Mixing bowl
Pastry cutter (optional)

INGREDIENTS

1 apple
2 ¼ cups all-purpose flour (or gluten-free flour blend)
½ cup sugar
1 tablespoon baking powder
1 teaspoon ground cinnamon
½ cup plus 2 tablespoons cold unsalted butter
½ teaspoon salt
½ cup heavy cream
½ cup applesauce
Extra flour for dusting

*Serve hot, slathered with butter or drizzled with **Cinnamon Icing**.*

STEPS

1. Preheat your oven to 375 degrees. Line a baking sheet with parchment paper.

2. Peel the apple and remove the core. Then chop the apple into cubes about ½ inch big.

3. In your mixing bowl, combine the flour, sugar, baking powder, and cinnamon.

4. Mash in the butter until you've got teeny bits of flour-coated butter. Use a pastry cutter, two forks, or your fingers—anything that gets the job done.

5. Add the salt, cream, applesauce, and diced apple. Mix it up! Warning: it will be *sticky!*

6. Next, sprinkle some extra flour onto the counter. Scoop out half of the dough onto the floured counter, then sprinkle more flour on top. Pat the dough into a 6-inch disk. Repeat with the second half of the dough to form a second disk.

7. Cut each disk in half, then in half again to make 4 equal pieces. Then cut each of those wedges in half to make 8 triangles. Then cut again. You'll have 16 tiny scones!

8. Place the scones onto the lined baking sheet. Bake for 15 to 20 minutes, until the little scones are puffed and golden.

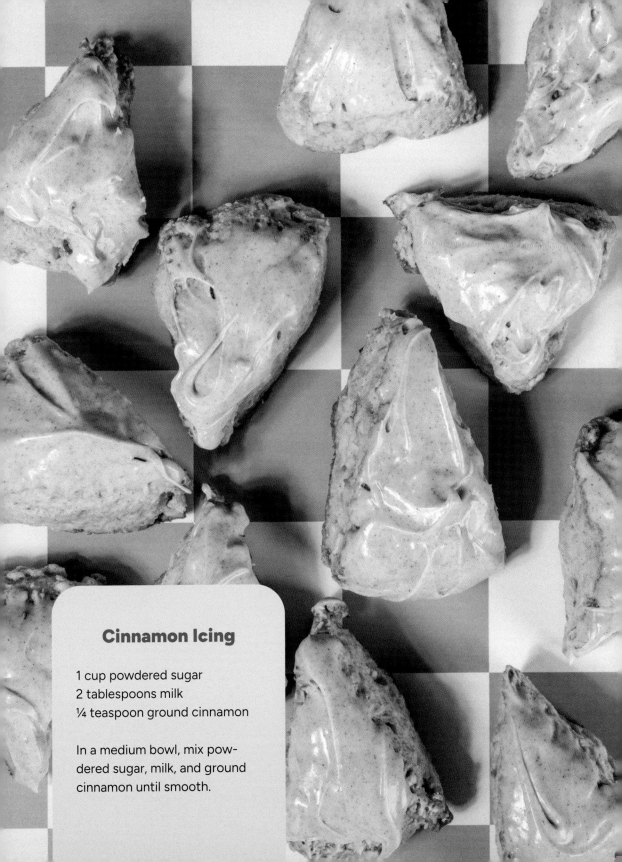

Cinnamon Icing

1 cup powdered sugar
2 tablespoons milk
¼ teaspoon ground cinnamon

In a medium bowl, mix powdered sugar, milk, and ground
cinnamon until smooth.

Layered Chocolate Cake with Cream Cheese Fluff

Prep time: 15 minutes | **Bake time:** 28 to 32 minutes
Makes 1 frosted double-layer cake, about 12 servings.

This cake is a lesson in creativity. Mixing a jar of marshmallow creme with cream cheese? A stroke of genius! This creamy, fluffy, marshmallowy goodness is the perfect partner to chocolate cake (or, really *any* cake)! Add your favorite sprinkles and you've got a party. Just remember, you can bake a cake any day of the week. No need to wait for a celebration. Every day is special with YOU!

SUPPLIES

2 (9-inch) cake pans
Parchment paper
Large mixing bowl
Medium mixing bowl
Whisk or hand mixer
Cake platter

INGREDIENTS

1 cup unsalted butter, melted
2 cups white sugar
½ cup plain Greek yogurt or sour cream
4 eggs
2 teaspoons vanilla extract
1 ¾ cups flour (*or gluten-free flour blend*)
1 cup cocoa powder
1 tablespoon baking powder
½ teaspoon salt
1 cup boiling water

Sprinkles (optional)

STEPS

1. Preheat your oven to 350 degrees, and line your pans with parchment paper.

2. In a large mixing bowl, mix the butter, sugar, yogurt or sour cream, eggs, and vanilla well.

3. Next add the dry ingredients: flour, cocoa powder, baking powder, and salt. Gently mix to combine.

4. Add the boiling water. Scrape the sides of the bowl and mix until smooth.

5. Pour half the batter into each pan, then bake for 28 to 32 minutes, until a toothpick comes out clean. Cool the cakes completely.

6. While the cakes bake, make **Cream Cheese Fluff**.

7. To assemble, set one cooled cake onto the platter and top with half the fluff. Spread the fluff to the edges of the cake.

8. Place the second cake on top. Spread the remaining fluff over the top of the cake. No need to frost the sides. Add some swirls with a spoon or butter knife to make it pretty. Add sprinkles for fun if you like!

Cream Cheese Fluff

1 (8-ounce) package cream cheese, softened
½ cup unsalted butter, softened
1 (7-ounce) container marshmallow creme
1 cup powdered sugar
½ teaspoon vanilla extract

In a medium bowl, mix the cream cheese and softened butter together until smooth. Add the marshmallow creme, powdered sugar, and vanilla. Scrape down the sides of the bowl and mix until smooth and creamy.

Use a ¼ cup measuring cup to neatly pour the batter into the muffin liners!

PUMPKIN MUFFINS

Prep time: 10 minutes | **Bake time:** 18 to 20 minutes per batch
Makes 18 muffins.

~~~~~~

Pumpkin bread, pumpkin cake, pumpkin pie, pumpkin muffins! These
tasty little treats are easy to make! You can have them for breakfast
or a snack, and they make a nice lunch box addition as well.

~~~~~~

SUPPLIES

18 muffin tin liners
Muffin tin
Hand mixer (optional)
Large mixing bowl

INGREDIENTS

½ cup unsalted butter, softened
2 cups packed brown sugar
2 tablespoons vegetable oil
3 eggs, room temperature
1 ½ cups canned pumpkin puree
2 teaspoons vanilla extract
½ teaspoon ground cinnamon
1 teaspoon salt
2 cups flour (*or gluten-free flour
    blend*)
1 tablespoon baking powder
½ teaspoon baking soda
½ cup full-fat buttermilk or plain
    Greek yogurt

STEPS

1. Preheat the oven to 350 degrees. Pop your muffin tin liners into the muffin tin.

2. With the hand mixer on low speed, combine the butter and brown sugar in your mixing bowl. Or use a nice big spoon!

3. Next up, mix in the oil.

4. Add the eggs one at a time, beating on low speed after each egg is added. If using a spoon, stir until the eggs are fully mixed in.

5. Now add the pumpkin, vanilla, cinnamon, and salt. Mix until just combined.

6. Add the flour, baking powder, and baking soda. Mix gently by hand until the flour just disappears.

7. Last, add the buttermilk or Greek yogurt and gently combine. Do not overmix.

8. Scoop your batter into the prepared muffin tin and bake for 18 to 20 minutes. Bake until a toothpick inserted comes out clean. Then remove the muffins in their liners to a cooling rack or towel laid out on the counter to cool. Bake the remainder of the batter in the same fashion as the first pan.

No-Bake Raspberry Parfait

Prep time: 10 minutes | **Fridge time:** 2+ hours
Makes 4 parfaits.

These cool and refreshing treats are perfect for warm weather or any time you want a quick sweet. They are also a perfect make-ahead dessert for parties or celebrations. Swap out the raspberry ingredients for other seasonal fruit flavors to make these in a fresh way throughout the year.

SUPPLIES

Hand mixer
Large bowl
Small bowl
4 small glasses or parfait cups

INGREDIENTS

2 cups heavy whipping cream
1 cup raspberry yogurt
½ cup powdered sugar
¾ cup raspberry jam
¼ cup water
12 crispy plain cookies, such as ladyfingers or butter cookies (gluten-free, if needed)
1 cup fresh raspberries

STEPS

1. Whip the cream, yogurt, and powdered sugar with the hand mixer in a nice big bowl until the mixture is thick and fluffy.

2. In a small bowl, stir together the raspberry jam and water until combined.

3. Now assemble the parfaits. Crumble a cookie into the bottom of each parfait cup. Add 1 tablespoon of the jam mixture over the top.

4. Add 2 to 3 spoonsful of your whipped cream mixture. The glass should be about half full.

5. Now for the second layer. Crumble another cookie on top of the cream and add another tablespoon of the raspberry jam mixture.

6. Spoon the rest of the cream evenly into the 4 cups.

7. Top with fresh raspberries and one more cookie. Chill these overnight or for at least 2 hours.

Campfire Oatmeal Cookies

Prep time: 10 minutes | **Bake time:** 12 minutes per batch
Makes about 32 cookies.

Bring the taste of a campfire inside with these cookies that taste
just like s'mores. These crisp cookies with bites of melty chocolate
and marshmallows will be your new favorite fall treat.

SUPPLIES

2 large baking sheets
Parchment paper
Large mixing bowl
Whisk or hand mixer

INGREDIENTS

1 cup unsalted butter, softened
1 cup dark brown sugar
¾ cup white sugar
2 eggs
2 teaspoons vanilla extract
1 ½ cups flour
¾ teaspoon baking powder
¾ teaspoon salt
¾ teaspoon ground cinnamon
1 heaping cup quick oats
1 cup broken graham cracker bits
1 cup chocolate chips
1 cup mini marshmallows

STEPS

1. Preheat the oven to 350 degrees. Line the baking sheets with parchment paper.

2. In the mixing bowl, mix the butter, brown sugar, and white sugar until fluffy.

3. Mix in the eggs and vanilla.

4. Stir in the flour, baking powder, salt, and cinnamon. Mix until just combined. Add the oats, cracker bits, chocolate chips, and marshmallows.

5. Use a dinner spoon to scoop balls of dough onto the baking sheets. Space the dough balls about 2 inches apart.

6. Bake for 12 minutes or until the cookies are no longer glossy on top and the edges are slightly golden.

7. Remove the *hot* baking sheets from the oven with an oven mitt. Slide the entire parchment paper off the sheets onto a heatproof counter, a cooling rack, or a dish towel.

8. These cookies like to spread out, so use a spatula to push the edges in and reshape to make the cookies rounder.

9. Repeat steps 5 through 8 with the rest of the dough.

Candy Chip Blondie Bars

Prep time: 15 minutes | **Bake time:** 28 to 35 minutes
Makes 24 (2-inch) blondie bars.

What's a blondie, you ask? Why, it's a brownie with *no* chocolate! But instead of skipping the chocolate completely, this recipe takes the typical vanilla blondie bar and sprinkles the chocolate back in with a burst of chips and colored candies. Sound good? Good! Let's *bake*!

SUPPLIES

Large mixing bowl
Hand mixer or whisk
9 x 13-inch baking pan

INGREDIENTS

1 cup unsalted butter, softened
1 cup packed dark brown sugar
1 cup white sugar
2 eggs
1 teaspoon vanilla extract
½ teaspoon salt
2 cups all-purpose flour (*or gluten-free flour blend*)
1 teaspoon baking powder
½ teaspoon baking soda
1 cup coated chocolate candies
½ cup chocolate chips

STEPS

1. Preheat your oven to 350 degrees, my friend!

2. In the large bowl, use a hand mixer or whisk to combine the butter, brown sugar, and white sugar until the batter is nice and smooth.

3. Add the eggs and mix again.

4. Next, add the vanilla and salt. Give it a nice mix.

5. Add the flour, baking powder, baking soda, candies, and chocolate chips. You guessed it! Mix again! Stir with a spoon or spatula until the dough is just combined, with no more flour streaks.

6. Now, dump that dough into your baking pan and press it evenly into the bottom, all the way to the edges. Get your hands in there if you want to!

7. Bake for 28 to 35 minutes. We like our bars on the gooey side. Bake longer for more crumbly bars.

8. If you can stand it, let the bars cool in the pan for 30 minutes before slicing them.

Mix gently at each step to keep the bars tender.
Too much mixing can create a tough blondie.

Happy Camper Hot Cocoa

Cook time: 10 minutes
Makes 1 quart, about 4 servings.

What does chilly weather taste like? Hot cocoa, of course! This recipe makes the creamiest, coziest cup of chocolate cheer you've ever had. It's perfect for wintertime, chilly evenings, and camping trips!

SUPPLIES

Large saucepan
Medium mixing bowl
Whisk or hand mixer

INGREDIENTS

2 cups whole milk
2 cups heavy cream or
    half-and-half
½ cup white sugar
½ cup unsweetened cocoa
    powder
½ teaspoon ground cinnamon
    (optional)
½ cup chopped dark chocolate
Pinch of sea salt
1 teaspoon vanilla extract
chocolate syrup (optional)

Your hot chocolate may look dappled due to the fat in the cream and chocolate. No problem! Smooth it out with a whisk, or enjoy it as is!

STEPS

1. In a large saucepan, combine all the cocoa ingredients.

2. Simmer and stir the cocoa gently over medium heat for about 10 minutes, until it's smooth and creamy and you don't see any more flecks of cocoa powder or chocolate. Be careful not to boil.

3. While the cocoa simmers, prepare **Soft Whipped Cream.**

4. Ask an adult to pour the hot cocoa into cups. Then add a scoop of whipped cream, and chocolate syrup if you wish, to each cup to serve.

Soft Whipped Cream

1 cup heavy cream
2 tablespoons white sugar
1 teaspoon vanilla extract
Pinch of sea salt

In a medium mixing bowl, whisk the cream, sugar, vanilla, and salt with a whisk or hand mixer until it becomes just firm enough to form a little hill when you lift out the whisk.

Pear-Nana Cake

Prep time: 15 minutes | **Bake time:** 35 to 40 minutes
Makes one 9 x 13-inch sheet cake, about 20 pieces.

Does your countertop fruit bowl have smooshy fruit in it? Well, this
cake is a wonderful way to use up those spotty bananas and pears!
You'll be so surprised at just how tasty this snack cake can be.

SUPPLIES

9 x 13-inch metal baking pan
Large mixing bowl
Hand mixer (optional)

INGREDIENTS

2 tablespoons butter for the
    pan
1 large or 2 small overripe pears
2 overripe bananas, peeled
2 eggs
½ cup plain yogurt
1 ½ cups white sugar
¼ cup molasses
1 teaspoon vanilla extract
2 cups flour (or gluten-free
    flour blend)
½ teaspoon ground cinnamon
½ teaspoon salt
2 teaspoons baking powder
½ teaspoon baking soda

STEPS

1. Preheat the oven to 350 degrees. Coat your 9 x 13-inch metal baking pan with butter.

2. Next, chop the pear with a butter knife. You can leave on the skin.

3. Then in a large mixing bowl, smash the peeled bananas and the pears until smooth. You can use a fork or the hand mixer.

4. Add the eggs. You may need some help to crack-a-lack those eggs open! Mix in the yogurt, sugar, molasses, and vanilla until completely combined.

5. Now, add the flour, cinnamon, salt, baking powder, and baking soda.

6. Give it all a good mix and pour it into the buttered baking pan.

7. Bake for 35 to 40 minutes or until the cake is set and no longer glossy.

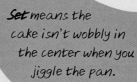

Set means the cake isn't wobbly in the center when you jiggle the pan.

INDEX

ABOUT THE AUTHOR AND PHOTOGRAPHER

Danielle Kartes is an author, recipe maven, and entrepreneur living near Seattle, Washington, with her photographer husband, Michael, and their two sweet boys.

Together the Karteses run their boutique food, lifestyle, and commercial photography business, Rustic Joyful Food. Rustic Joyful Food promotes loving your life right where you are, no matter where you are, and creating beautiful, delicious food that's fuss-free with whatever you have available to you.

Danielle is driven by her love for Jesus, her family, and happy accidents in the kitchen. She has written and published four cookbooks, seven children's books, and one devotional memoir. Danielle appears often on national television and is a regular culinary contributor to *The Kelly Clarkson Show.*